Selective Bibliography
for the Study of
English and American Literature

SELECTIVE BIBLIOGRAPHY
for the Study of
English and American
Literature

SECOND EDITION

by
RICHARD D. ALTICK
and
ANDREW WRIGHT

The Macmillan Company, New York
Collier-Macmillan Limited, London

First Printing

Library of Congress catalog card number: 63-13570

The Macmillan Company, New York
Collier-Macmillan Canada, Ltd., Toronto, Ontario
Divisions of The Crowell-Collier Publishing Company

Printed in the United States of America

Preface to the Second Edition

In the three years since the first edition of this book went to the printer, so many bibliographies and other works important to literary study have been published that a thorough revision has become necessary. Of the five hundred numbered entries, fifty-five are new, and forty-two more have been altered to take account of new editions, supplementary volumes, and the like. It is expected that similar revised editions will appear every few years.

Valuable suggestions for the improvement of the book have been made by a number of its users. Several additions and amendments to the "Glossary of Useful Terms" are the contribution of Professors Lester A. Beaurline and Matthew J. Bruccoli.

March 1963.

Preface

The chief purpose of this compilation is to provide students of English and American literature with a convenient and reasonably authoritative guide to research materials. It is highly selective; many items which have appeared in similar handbooks have been rejected as being obsolete, or untrustworthy, or simply not valuable enough for the student to bother with. We have tried always to keep in mind the needs of today's scholars, which in some ways are different from the needs of preceding generations. Thus, the interests and approaches of practicing scholars seem no longer to justify including a "classic" work like Petzholdt's *Bibliotheca Bibliographica* (published in 1866) among the bibliographies every student should know. Accordingly, we have sought to include only those bibliographies and reference works which are actually used—and usable—by modern scholars. Desire for conciseness has required the omission of many items that have potential usefulness at some point in a given course of investigation, but these can easily be found through the more comprehensive guides which we do include. On the other hand, we have had to list a certain number of inferior works: these cover, however sparsely, ground that would otherwise remain bare. The principle underlying our selection has always been that of Roger Williams, in *A Key into the Language of America* (1643): "A Little *Key* may open a *Box*, where lies a *bunch* of *Keyes*." The following pages contain most of the all-important "little" keys.

In addition to listing the books which are indispensable to any program of independent research, whether for a graduate seminar report, a dissertation, or a post-doctoral project, we have had several other purposes in mind. One is to offer a list—again, highly selective—of histories of English and American literature, both general and specialized (that is, confined to specific periods or types). The climate of academic opinion in late years has been somewhat unfavorable to the use of such books by graduate students. But because leisure for the reading of the actual texts of all literary masterpieces is available only in some timeless Utopia, and, on the other hand, the general examination that is the gateway to candidacy for the Ph.D. may range over a thousand years of literary history, a judicious, discriminating use of books like Baugh and Spiller would seem to be not only legitimate but unavoidable. Books *about* literature can be grossly misused by the slothful and the unscrupulous; but so can telephone directories, whose usefulness and legality remain unimpaired by their occasional services to people needing bookmakers. The titles listed here happen to be those which we consider the best in their various fields. When the best is excellent, we have generally allowed no remark of ours, beyond what may be inferred from the inclusion of the book, to distract the reader; when the best is none too good, we have sometimes felt obliged to comment on the book's shortcomings.

Another concern has been to suggest works which are useful for occasional, incidental reference—to supply biographical data, the details of a Greek myth, the essential information about existentialism, and so on. Here, as elsewhere, we have sought to enable the student to become his own reference librarian, thus releasing those hard-working professional servants of the public for more esoteric pursuits. Every scholar worthy of the name, no matter how many years separate him from the Ph.D. in one direction or the other, must develop to a high degree the all-essential qualities of independence and ingenuity. He should know his way around the bailiwick of miscellaneous bibliography so well that only seldom should he have to enlist the aid of a librarian. Hence this compilation is designed to help him find the answers to many kinds of "reference" questions.

Recognizing as we do that literary studies in recent years have tended to spill into other causeways, we have included a certain number of indispensable items in fields that are not primarily literary. We have, for instance, listed the most important aids to historical and biographical research. Similarly there are sections on social and intellectual history. There is also a list of works which, while they resist classification, are of great importance to any student of literature. Such books as John Livingston Lowes's *The Road to Xanadu* and Erich Auerbach's *Mimesis* and Henry Nash Smith's

Virgin Land appear in a separate section which we have called
"Some Books Every Student of Literature Should Read." Altogether,
we have attempted to construct a well-rounded *vade mecum* to literary studies, in which every area of concern to the graduate student
and the mature scholar has been, at least in some measure, treated.

Believing that in a book of this sort the arrangement should be
determined by common sense rather than a pedantic passion for
universal consistency, we have let the internal logic of each section
decide the order of the entries. Thus the histories of literature appear, within the various subcategories, in order of first publication;
but in the sections on cultural and intellectual history and on retro-
spective national bibliographies, for example, the arrangement, after
the listing of general works, is by specific periods covered. A third
kind of arrangement appears in the section on American libraries.
Here the order is geographical, beginning in New England and
progressing westward. In brief, our aim has been to arrange the items
as usefully as possible, and to make clear, by our choice of ordering,
the relationship the various items in each category bear to one another.

In the main body of the book the items are numbered. We have
omitted four or five numbers after each section and subsection, so
that new titles can conveniently be inserted. In citing edited works,
the form of our entry has been determined by the way the work is
usually referred to—whether by title or by editor's name. Authors'
names are regularly given as they appear on title pages. Subtitles
are omitted unless they say something useful. Occasionally, where
knowledge of the age of a book is of special pertinence, we have
indicated the date of its first publication as well as that of the newest
edition. Only one place of publication is given for each title. Thus
in style as in arrangement we have tried to be sufficiently detailed,
but in such a way as to be desirably short-winded.

R.D.A.
A.W.

Contents

On the Use of Scholarly Tools

No bibliography, indeed no work of reference, is perfect; but some are less perfect than others. All the books listed here are useful in one kind of research or another, and some are absolutely indispensable in their various areas of interest. But to use them undiscriminatingly, without clear understanding of what they have and what they do not have, where they excel and where they fall short, is to waste hours and weeks of precious time.

Before using any reference tool, the student should carefully examine it, to discover not only its avowed but also its unacknowledged strengths, weaknesses, and peculiarities. He should keep in mind the possibility that he will have to refer to the book scores of times in the next year or two. His examination should therefore be careful enough to be permanently useful. The time he spends in such a preliminary survey is nearly always repaid, many times over, in the efficiency with which he can then use the book, in the elimination of wasted time (looking for material that simply isn't there), and in the avoidance of the booby trap of erroneous or incomplete information. The following pages are designed to suggest some of the things the student should keep in mind as he encounters a research tool for the first time. The advice is, of course, not exhaustive. But it at least implies the spirit—a mingling of respect and skepticism—in which all such first meetings should be managed.

1. *The front matter.* What are the stated <u>purposes</u> and stated <u>limits</u> of the work? These can seldom be compressed into the few words of a subtitle; they must be <u>explained in detail in a preface or introduction</u>. A single sentence may quickly reveal that the book does not contain the kind of material for which one is looking. Without reading the introduction, it is impossible to know that Besterman's *World Bibliography of Bibliographies* (**502**)* excludes a large

---

* The bold-face figures in parentheses refer to the numbered items in the main body of this book.

class of bibliographies: those which were included in larger works but were never issued separately. But not all introductions are candid and accurate in their description of a book's scope and achievement. Some, like the magnificently florid overture to Allibone's *Critical Dictionary of English Literature* (39)—a work which is the very reverse of critical as we now understand the term—, are nothing more than unblushing blurbs; others, perhaps more modest in tone, are nevertheless only statements of pious intent. That is why it is always necessary to check up on the promises found in the front matter by actually testing the work and consulting expert opinion. Many reference works are not what they seem or pretend or would like to be.

In a multi-volume work, published over a considerable period of time, the later volumes may have separate introductions which announce important shifts in policy and scope. In the course of publication Courtney's *Register of National Bibliography* (503) ceased to be "national" and began to include non-British items. Sabin's *Bibliotheca Americana* (821) underwent successive contractions of coverage in the later stages of compilation, and one should never use a given volume without first consulting the introduction in Volume XXIX to discover what limitations were in effect at that particular point. Occasionally, the introductory matter indispensable for efficient use of a work may not appear in the place where one would expect to find it. In Sir Walter Greg's *Bibliography of the English Printed Drama* (411), for instance, it is found in Volume IV.

2. *The book's age.* Is it of recent origin, according to the date of publication? The date on the title page may be misleading, for it may merely represent the date of a fresh printing without change of content. Some copies of Millett's *Contemporary British Literature* (385) have an imprint date of 1950, but the book was last revised in 1935. Furthermore, was the book really up-to-date when published? Some scholarly books may await publication for years, and during the interval between completion and publication the fatigued author may neglect to add recent materials to his manuscript. It has been remarked, truly, that every bibliography is out of date before it is published—the present one doubtless is no exception—but it is desirable to know *how* dated every book really is. And even within a single work there may be considerable discrepancy. The *CBEL* (374) appeared in 1941, but the individual sections were completed

anywhere from two to ten years earlier. The section on the Oxford Movement (III, 854-55) contains nothing written on the subject after 1930, thus missing the large amount of important material published in the centenary year, 1933; the Drayton section (I, 423-25) stops at 1931. When the Supplement (published 1957) was prepared, the dovetailing of the continuations with the original sections was not always perfect, with the result that in the record of modern scholarship and criticism on some authors there may be a gap of several years between where the original compiler left off and where his successor began.

As a very general rule, it is true that a newer book is preferable to an older one; but there are so many exceptions and qualifications that one must examine each case on its own merits. The newer book published in 1960 may indisputably have the benefit of thirty more years' research than an older one dated 1930; but it may also be less detailed and less reliable. Thus sometimes the work that is superficially "obsolete" may prove by far the more fruitful source to consult. For some purposes the eleventh edition of the *Encyclopædia Britannica* (**542**) is better than the more recent, streamlined ones. Even books as old as Watt's *Bibliotheca Britannica*, 1824 (**511**), Lowndes's *Bibliographer's Manual*, 1857-64 (**371**), and Brunet's *Manuel du libraire et de l'amateur de livres*, 1860-80 (**513**) have their occasional usefulness today. Allibone, published 1858-91, has a wealth of out-of-the-way information on third- and tenth-rate writers that is collected nowhere else. So the rule should be: Scorn not the older book just because it is old. The newest book may indeed say all there is to be said on the subject—but not just because it is new.

Many reference books go through one or more revisions. Some revisions are so extensive that the preceding editions are entirely superseded. The first edition of Besterman, dated 1939-40, was lamentably incomplete, one reason being that it did not draw upon the extensive bibliographical collections of the Library of Congress. The second, dated 1947-49, was bigger and better, but suffered from the difficulties the bibliographer inevitably faced as a result of the war and its aftermath. The "third and final" edition, 1955-56, containing 80,000 entries as against the first edition's 42,000, is what the book should have been in the first place. Again, the hand lists of plays that were an important feature of Nicoll's original series of volumes on the British drama from 1660 onward were very incomplete. These should now be consulted in their considerably expanded form, in the revised edition of the series (173).

"Revision" does not necessarily imply mere expansion, correction, and bringing up to date. It may also mean more or less sweeping changes of content. Certain articles that appear in one edition of that fascinating grab bag of historical odds and ends, *Haydn's Dictionary of Dates* (882), are missing from the next, and articles on different topics appear instead. Similarly, the current editions of Millett's two bibliographies of "contemporary" British and American literature (385 and 432) omit scores of literary figures who appeared in the earlier ones, edited by Manly and Rickert, but whose celebrity proved impermanent. To obtain bibliographical information on many minor writers of the period 1900-1930, therefore, one must still refer to those "obsolete" Manly-Rickert volumes.

3. *Indexes.* To the traveler along the reference shelves, there is no more refreshing experience than to open a volume and behold a large, well-printed, and adequately subdivided index. But the oasis may prove a brackish mirage if the indexing turns out to be defective. A quick and fairly accurate way of finding out whether an index may be used with confidence is to pick eight or ten names or subjects at random in the body of the book—not major references, but quite incidental ones, perhaps some occurring in lengthy lists— and then check on their accurate inclusion in the index. The conclusion to be drawn if none of them is there, or if some are there and others aren't, is obvious. Occasionally indexes are limited arbitrarily to certain kinds of material. In the indispensable Stationers' Register (784), for example, everybody connected with the printing and bookselling trades is indexed, but not the authors or titles of the thousands of books entered in the register.

If the work is in more than one volume, one must be sure to determine whether there is a reliable master index to the whole set, or whether each volume is indexed separately. A third possibility is that the indexing is done on some less common plan, such as one index for every two or three volumes. Here a knowledge of the publishing history of the set would prove valuable. It may never be assumed that a work lacks an index simply because the index is not in the usual place, at the end; in Bonamy Dobrée's six-volume edition of Lord Chesterfield's letters, published in 1932, the index to the whole set occurs in Volume I.

If a desired heading does not appear in an index, it always pays to look under various synonyms. Until fairly recently, most indexing was done on quite arbitrary and individualistic principles, so that if one failed to guess the exact word the indexer chose to designate a certain subject, he quite possibly would not find the references he was looking for. Relatively few older books possess the elaborate and efficient system of cross-references to which the publications of the H. W. Wilson Company (*Readers' Guide, International Index, Bibliographic Index*, etc.) have accustomed present-day researchers. The predecessor of these modern compilations, Poole's guide to nineteenth-century periodicals (**680**), scatters articles on a single broad subject under several headings, depending usually on the wording of the title. Thus, as the historian of the Wilson indexes reminds us, for a bibliography on the labor movement, Poole must be consulted under Labor, Associations of; Labor, Organized; Labor Associations; Labor Unions; Trade-Unionism; and Trade-Unions. On alcoholism one must look under not only that word but also under Alcoholic Excesses, the Drink Question, Drunkards, Drunkenness, Inebriates, Inebriety, Intemperance, Liquor, and Temperance.

In serial publications, comprehensive indexes of authors and titles are often provided at the end of a certain number of volumes. We have usually indicated the existence of such indexes in our entries for various periodicals. For a further useful guide, see Daniel C. Haskell, *A Check List of Cumulative Indexes to Individual Periodicals in the New York Public Library* (New York, 1942). One additional note: In the indexes to individual volumes and runs of some nineteenth-century periodicals, the alphabetization, once the initial letter of the word has been passed, is unpredictable, to say the least. LO may precede LE, and LA follow LI, with maddening insouciance.

4. *Plan.* Some works contain several alphabets or parts, each of which must be consulted in quest of a certain bit of information. There may be, for example, separate author, title, and subject alphabets. Or, as in the case of Peddie's *Subject Index* (**521**), each of four volumes may contain a complete alphabet, as well as a brief supplementary one, making a total of eight to be consulted. Courtney's *Register* (**503**) has two alphabets: the first extending over Volumes I and II, the second in Volume III. Thus the hasty student, assuming that Peddie and Courtney have amassed all entries for the letter B

in one place, is in danger of missing the very material for which he
is searching. Again, to establish whether or not a certain rare piece
of Americana is in the Library of Congress, one cannot stop with the
main LC *Catalog of Books* (313); there are also several later alphabets to consult, in volumes of the *Catalog* published since 1946.
(And, as a matter of fact, failure to find the item desired in any
volume of the LC *Catalog* is not conclusive proof that the LC does
not have it; for some very rare items, LC cards have never been
printed. On the other hand, the LC *Catalog* also contains entries for
some books which are owned by other libraries but not by the Library of Congress itself.)

Some important bibliographical tools have other peculiarities of
arrangement which must be understood before they can be satis-
factorily used. In the Stationers' Register, a verbatim transcript of
various types of records of the Stationers' Company extending over
many decades, data relating to the publishing history of a certain
book, or the dealings of a bookseller, may have to be assembled
from several widely separated places. In Wells's *Manual of the Writings in Middle English* (381) the main volume is divided into two
parts, one containing substantive information (dates, authorship,
sources, contents, etc. of literary works) and the other containing
bibliographical references. This division is maintained throughout
the nine supplements, and the reference system by which the supplements are tied to each other and to the parent volume calls for
patient mastery before use. Perhaps most important of all, the
arrangement of the "old" British Museum *Catalogue of Printed
Books* (336) is so tricky (alphabetization combining I and J, U
and V; dazzlingly whimsical handling of anonymous and pseudonymous titles; lumping of masses of titles under broad headings like
"Academies") that the student seeking to avoid frustration and out-
right betrayal is required to familiarize himself with the rules set
forth in the pamphlet listed under **336.**

5. *Accuracy.* A reference work that is inconveniently arranged is
a nuisance, but with persistence it may be forced to yield up its
quota of information. A work that is unreliable, however, presents
problems that are both more subtle and more sinister. If the data the
scholar collects are inaccurate, the whole process of research is futile.

The sources and occasions of error in reference books, needless
to say, are manifold. From the modern scholarly point of view,

among the most culpable of sins is the uncritical adoption of somebody else's "facts." This, apart from justifiable indignation over the
chaotic arrangement, is the main charge against W. Carew Hazlitt's
series of bibliographies of pre-1700 English literature (383). Especially in the earliest volumes, Hazlitt depended too freely on the
kindness of friends at Oxford and Cambridge, who favored him with
much imprecise information that he never bothered to verify. (It
is also said that much of Hazlitt's undependability can be traced to
his habit of making notes on the backs of old envelopes, but since
this is a standard libel among scholars, it may be no more true
of Hazlitt than of some other bibliographers.) Block's bibliography
of the English novel (422) likewise has been severely criticized for
its reliance on secondary sources such as the British Museum Catalogue and booksellers' catalogues, without any systematic attempt
to examine the books themselves. Nowadays the best practice requires that, except in the most extraordinary circumstances, the
bibliographer *see* every book he lists; otherwise there is always the
chance that his pages will harbor a few bibliographical ghosts.
Blanck's great new *Bibliography of American Literature* (430) is
being constructed on that admirable principle. A corollary rule requires that the student transcribe the author, title, and publishing
information of any book he cites from the title page itself, rather
than from any bibliographical reference. Some reference books are
seriously unreliable in their presentation of titles. In Poole's *Index*,
for example, the titles of some periodical articles are not identical
with those found in the magazines themselves, and in Malclès' *Les
Sources du travail bibliographique* (494) some of the standard works
included in the present handbook are incorrectly listed. It would be
interesting to discover how many respected bibliographies, including the *CBEL* itself (III, 250), list a two-volume work entitled *The
Letters of Robert Browning and Elizabeth Barrett Browning*. There
is no such book. The reference, no doubt, is to a well-known book
whose title page actually reads *The Letters of Robert Browning and
Elizabeth Barrett Barrett*.

How can the student guard against being misled by his reference
sources? One way is to find out the editor's or compiler's general
reputation for dependability. Unfortunately there is no bibliographical Dun and Bradstreet that lists people's scholarly standing. All one
can do is to be constantly alert for remarks made in other books or

dropped by one's teachers in lectures or seminar discussions. By keeping his eyes and ears open, the student of Elizabethan drama, for instance, will soon become aware that F. G. Fleay (1831-1909) is notorious for his wild surmises, and that to cite him as a sole authority for any statement is an act of naiveté. In such works as Winchell's *Guide to Reference Books* (495), critical evaluations are made of many of the books listed here. But the standards by which professional librarians judge the dependability of reference books are, necessarily, more lenient than those employed by specialists in any field of learning; so that many a book which is perfectly service-able for the ordinary library patron is not reliable enough for the stern requirements of the expert.

Another way to learn the standing of a research tool, particu-larly a specialized one in the field of literary scholarship, is to look up the scholarly reviews. Everyone who has frequent occasion to use the *CBEL* would do well to consult a few of the extensive re-views that followed its publication. Among the most informative are those in the *TLS*, December 21 and 28, 1940, pp. 648, 660; *PQ*, XXI (1942), 251-56; *MP*, XXXIX (1941/2), 303-12; *MLN*, LVII (1942), 285-88; *RES*, XVII (1941), 490-94, and *The Library*, 4th ser., XXII (1942), 250-55. In another field of interest, a survey of the reviews of Spiller's *Literary History of the United States* (187) reveals the diversity of opinion that a single work can evoke, as well as the variety of considerations that govern such opinion. See, for example, the *Kenyon Review*, XI (1949), 500-06; *American Quar-terly*, I (1949), 169-83; *MLN*, LXV (1950), 258-61; and *American Literature*, XXI (1949/50), 489-92.

6. *Thoroughness and bias.* Relatively few research tools approach absolute exhaustiveness on their chosen subject. Thus it is always desirable to know, either from the editors' explicit statements or by inference from the contents, the circumstances that have limited a work's scope or affected its emphasis. Many bibliographies of indi-vidual authors or of specific types have been based, not upon a wide-ranging canvass of many libraries, but upon a single collection. Perhaps the most famous recent example of this is the sumptuous catalogue of "nineteenth-century" (actually in great part Victorian) fiction by Michael Sadleir (423), which, as the subtitle says, is based on his own collection. Valuable though the two volumes are, they cannot be regarded as exhaustive or comprehensive, since their con-

tents were determined by Sadleir's personal tastes as a collector and his luck in acquiring copies of books notoriously difficult to collect.

Any work to which many hands contribute is bound to be uneven. The disproportion between many sections of the *CBEL* is well known. The fact that Spenser occupies only five columns, as against Shakespeare's 136, is hardly a fair measure of the two poets' respective importance; neither is it a measure of the work done on Spenser. Some sections of the *CBEL*, such as those on the history of printing and publishing and on periodicals, are among the best available bibliographical guides to their subjects. Others are so highly selective, or even capricious, as to be virtually worthless for the purposes of serious research. As is true of Spiller's *Literary History* and numerous other collaborative enterprises, the value of any particular section depends on the conscientiousness and expertness of the man or woman who produced it.

National origin accounts for considerable imbalance in certain reference works. *The Year's Work in English Studies* (**454**), which has a staff of British contributors, often neglects American scholarly productions of distinctly greater importance than some British works that receive more extended treatment. Mlle. Malclès places greatest stress on the bibliographical and reference tools of European countries, particularly France, while Miss Winchell emphasizes American ones—in both cases an understandable, and in practical terms entirely defensible, bias. Less defensible, perhaps, is the heavy predominance of the work of German scholars and critics in books like Hans Eppelsheimer's *Handbuch der Weltliteratur*. In any event, where there is a choice of sources to be consulted, one must take into account the likelihood that the fullest and most authoritative treatment of materials pertaining to a certain country will be found in a reference work originating there. This is less true, of course, in the field of literary studies, where so many of the "standard" books on English literature have been produced by Americans.

Again, there is the question of the audience or market for which the work was intended. The variety of author bibliographies illustrates the point. Some bibliographies of this kind were compiled primarily to help librarians strengthen their collections of the authors' works. They are therefore little more than "check lists," and have relatively minor research usefulness. Others were designed especially for collectors, many of whom are sentimentalists rather than scholars. Sometimes they contain much valuable material, but to find the grain requires much sifting out of chaff. (An example is William Miller's voluminous *The Dickens Student and Collector* [Cambridge, Mass., 1946], which is uncritical in the extreme and disfigured by many errors.) In a similar category are author bibliographies compiled by booksellers. These are often more accurately described as catalogues of individual collections which the dealer has either amassed himself or purchased *en bloc.* Obviously they are not exhaustive; and their emphasis consistently is on the features of the books or manuscripts which enhance their market value—features that are not always those which interest the scholar. Finally, there are author bibliographies intended specifically for scholarly use, compiled by persons who, at least theoretically, know what scholars need and want. Abstractly considered, these should always be the most valuable kind of reference tool. But in practice such is not always the case, simply because, as everywhere else in life, the quality of performance varies from person to person.

And so we return to the point from which we started: No single book recorded in the following pages is perfect, because no man or combination of men is infallible. The ultimate worth of any reference work depends on its maker's devotion, intelligence, erudition, and access to materials, and above all on the degree to which he has been able to harness these advantages to produce a work that is at once authoritative and convenient to use. It is not a simple task for the student to estimate how successful the compiler has been. But the more shrewdly he evaluates every book he uses, the more efficient and fruitful his own program of research will turn out to be.

SOME ABBREVIATIONS COMMONLY USED BY LITERARY SCHOLARS

For an exhaustive list of abbreviations of periodicals, see the annual bibliography number of *PMLA*.

AL	*American Literature*
BM	The British Museum
CBEL	*The Cambridge Bibliography of English Literature*
CBI	*Cumulative Book Index*
DAB	*Dictionary of American Biography*
DAE	*A Dictionary of American English*
DNB	*Dictionary of National Biography*
ELH	*ELH: A Journal of English Literary History**
JEGP	*Journal of English and Germanic Philology*
JHI	*Journal of the History of Ideas*
LC	The Library of Congress
LHUS	*Literary History of the United States*
MHRA	The Modern Humanities Research Association
MLA	The Modern Language Association of America
MLN	*Modern Language Notes*
MLQ	*Modern Language Quarterly*
MLR	*Modern Language Review*
MP	*Modern Philology*
NED	*A New English Dictionary* [also called *Oxford English Dictionary* and abbreviated *OED*]
N&Q	*Notes and Queries*
OED	*Oxford English Dictionary* [also abbreviated *NED*]
PBSA	*Papers of the Bibliographical Society of America*
PMLA	*Publications of the Modern Language Association of America***
PQ	*Philological Quarterly*
PRO	The Public Record Office (London)
RES	*Review of English Studies*
SP	*Studies in Philology*
STC	*Short-Title Catalogue*
TLS	*The* [London] *Times Literary Supplement*
ULS	*Union List of Serials*
YWES	*The Year's Work in English Studies*

* In 1956 the subtitle was dropped.

** The actual title is *PMLA: Publications of the Modern Language Association of America.*

THE SCOPE, AIMS, AND METHODS OF
LITERARY SCHOLARSHIP

1 WELLEK, RENÉ, and AUSTIN WARREN. Theory of Literature. New York, 1949.

2 ALTICK, RICHARD D. The Scholar Adventurers. New York, 1950.

3 SHERBURN, GEORGE. "Words That Intimidate." *PMLA*, LXV (1950), No. 1, pp. 3-12.

4 "The Aims, Methods, and Materials of Research in the Modern Languages and Literatures." *PMLA*, LXVII (1952), No. 6, pp. 3-37.

5 JONES, HOWARD MUMFORD. One Great Society: Humane Learning in the United States. New York, 1959.

   See especially Chapters 6, 7, and 11.

6 WHALLEY, GEORGE. "Scholarship and Criticism." University of Toronto Quarterly, XXIX (1959), 33-45.

7 BUSH, DOUGLAS. "Literary Scholarship and Criticism." Liberal Education, XLVII (1961), 207-28.

BIBLIOGRAPHICAL HANDBOOKS

13 BOND, DONALD F. A Reference Guide to English Studies. Chicago, 1962.

   "A revision of the Bibliographical Guide to English Studies by Tom Peete Cross" [10th ed. Chicago, 1951].

14 SPARGO, JOHN WEBSTER. A Bibliographical Manual for Students of the Language and Literature of England and the United States. 2nd ed. Chicago, 1941.

   The 3rd edition (1956) is inferior to the preceding editions.

15 KENNEDY, ARTHUR G. A Concise Bibliography for Students of English. 3rd ed. Stanford, 1954.

> The fourth edition of the book (edited by Donald B. Sands, 1960) contains three times as many titles as its predecessors.

THE TECHNIQUES OF RESEARCH

22 MORIZE, ANDRÉ. Problems and Methods of Literary History. Boston, 1922.

23 BARZUN, JACQUES, and HENRY F. GRAFF. The Modern Researcher. New York, 1957.

> See Part 2.

SCHOLARLY STYLE

29 McKERROW, R. B. "Form and Matter in the Publication of Research." *RES*, XVI (1940), 116-21.

> Reprinted in *PMLA*, LXV (1950), No. 3, pp. 3-8.

30 UNIVERSITY OF CHICAGO PRESS. A Manual of Style. 11th ed. Chicago, 1949.

31 SILVER, HENRY M. "Putting It on Paper." *PMLA*, LXV (1950), No. 3, pp. 9-20.

32 The MLA Style Sheet, compiled by William Riley Parker. Revised ed. New York, 1954.

(23) BARZUN, JACQUES, and HENRY F. GRAFF. The Modern Researcher. New York, 1957.

> See Part 3.

LITERARY ENCYCLOPEDIAS AND HANDBOOKS

English and American

39 ALLIBONE, S. AUSTIN. A Critical Dictionary of English Literature and British and American Authors. 3 vols. Philadelphia, 1858-71. Supplement. 2 vols. Philadelphia, 1891.

40 [GHOSH, J. C.] Annals of English Literature 1475-1950. 2nd ed. [revised by R. W. Chapman et al.] Oxford, 1961.

41 The Oxford Companion to English Literature, ed. Paul Harvey. 3rd ed. Oxford, 1946.

42 The New Century Handbook of English Literature, ed. Clarence L. Barnhart. New York, 1956.

43 The Oxford Companion to American Literature, ed. James D. Hart. 3rd ed. New York, 1956.

44 BURKE, W. J., and WILL D. HOWE. American Authors and Books 1640 to the Present Day. Revised ed. New York, 1962.

General, Classical, and Modern European

49 SHIPLEY, JOSEPH T. Encyclopedia of Literature. 2 vols. New York, 1946.

50 ———. Dictionary of World Literature. Revised ed. New York, 1953.

51 Cassell's Encyclopaedia of World Literature, ed. S. H. Steinberg. 2 vols. New York, 1954.
English title: Cassell's Encyclopaedia of Literature.

52 THOMPSON, STITH. Motif-Index of Folk-Literature. Revised ed. 6 vols. Bloomington, 1955-58.

53 Funk & Wagnalls Standard Dictionary of Folklore, Mythology and Legend, ed. Maria Leach and Jerome Fried. 2 vols. New York, 1949-50.

54 ATKINS, J. W. H. Literary Criticism in Antiquity. 2 vols. Cambridge, 1934.

55 THOMSON, J. A. K. The Classical Background of English Literature. London, 1948.

56 The Oxford Classical Dictionary, ed. M. Cary et al. Oxford, 1949.

57 HIGHET, GILBERT. The Classical Tradition: Greek and Roman Influences on Western Literature. Oxford, 1949.

58 GRAVES, ROBERT. The Greek Myths. 2 vols. London, 1955.

59 HADAS, MOSES. Ancilla to Classical Reading. New York, 1954.

60 The New Century Classical Handbook, ed. Catherine B. Avery. New York, 1962.

61 Répertoire chronologique des littératures modernes, ed. Paul Van Tieghem. Paris, 1935-37.

> See also ANTONY BRETT-JAMES, The Triple Stream: Four Centuries of English, French, and German Literature, 1531-1930 (Cambridge, 1953).

62 Columbia Dictionary of Modern European Literature, ed. Horatio Smith. New York, 1947.

63 The Oxford Companion to French Literature, ed. Paul Harvey and J. E. Heseltine. Oxford, 1959.

64 The Oxford Companion to the Theatre, ed. Phyllis Hartnoll. 2nd ed. London, 1957.

ENGLISH LITERATURE: General Histories

70 LEGOUIS, EMILE, and LOUIS CAZAMIAN. A History of English Literature. 2 vols. London, 1926-27.

> Revised edition in one volume, 1954.

71 WILSON, F. P., and BONAMY DOBRÉE, eds. Oxford History of English Literature. Oxford, 1945- .

> Of a projected fourteen volumes, five have been published; these are listed separately below (**90, 91, 99, 101, 110**).

72 BAUGH, ALBERT C., et al. A Literary History of England. New York, 1948.

> Also published in four volumes.

73 CRAIG, HARDIN, et al. A History of English Literature. New York, 1950.

ENGLISH LITERATURE: Period Histories

Anglo-Saxon Period

81 KER, W. P. Epic and Romance. 2nd ed. London, 1908.

82 KENNEDY, CHARLES W. The Earliest English Poetry. New York, 1943.

Middle English Period

88 KER, W. P.   English Literature Mediaeval. London, 1912.

89 LEWIS, C. S.   The Allegory of Love: A Study in Medieval Tradition. Revised ed. London, 1938.

90 CHAMBERS, E. K.   English Literature at the Close of the Middle Ages. (Oxford History of English Literature, Vol. II, Part 2.) Oxford, 1945.
Reprinted with corrections, 1947.

91 BENNETT, H. S. Chaucer and the Fifteenth Century. (Oxford History of English Literature, Vol. II, Part 1.) Oxford, 1947.

92 KANE, GEORGE.   Middle English Literature: A Critical Study of the Romances, the Religious Lyrics, Piers Plowman. London, 1951.

93 LOOMIS, ROGER SHERMAN, ed. Arthurian Literature in the Middle Ages: A Collaborative History. Oxford, 1959.

The Renaissance

98 GRIERSON, HERBERT J. C.   Cross Currents in English Literature of the Seventeenth Century. London, 1929.

99 BUSH, DOUGLAS.   English Literature in the Earlier Seventeenth Century, 1600-1660. (Oxford History of English Literature, Vol. V.) 2nd ed. Oxford, 1962.

100 WEDGWOOD, C. V.   Seventeenth-Century English Literature. London, 1950.

101 LEWIS, C. S.   English Literature in the Sixteenth Century Excluding Drama. (Oxford History of English Literature, Vol. III.) Oxford, 1954.

The Restoration and Eighteenth Century

107 STEPHEN, LESLIE.   English Literature and Society in the Eighteenth Century. London, 1904.

108 ELTON, OLIVER.   A Survey of English Literature, 1730-1780. 2 vols. London, 1928.

109   SHERBURN, GEORGE.   The Restoration and Eighteenth Century
      (1660-1789). (Baugh, A Literary History of England [72], Vol.
      III.) New York, 1948.

110   DOBRÉE, BONAMY.   English Literature in the Earlier Eight-
      eenth Century. (Oxford History of English Literature, Vol.
      VII.) Oxford, 1959.

The Nineteenth Century

116   ELTON, OLIVER.   A Survey of English Literature, 1780-1830.
      2 vols. London, 1912.

117   ———.   A Survey of English Literature, 1830-1880. 2 vols.
      London, 1920.

118   BUCKLEY, JEROME HAMILTON.   The Victorian Temper. Cam-
      bridge, Mass., 1951.

The Twentieth Century

123   TINDALL, WILLIAM YORK.   Forces in Modern British Litera-
      ture, 1885-1956. New York, 1956.

124   DAICHES, DAVID.   The Present Age After 1920. (Introductions
      to English Literature, Vol. V.) London, 1958.

ENGLISH LITERATURE: Special Topics

Linguistics

130   GLEASON, H. A., Jr.   An Introduction to Descriptive Linguis-
      tics. Revised ed. New York, 1961.

131   BAUGH, ALBERT C.   A History of the English Language. 2nd
      ed. New York, 1957.

132   BLOOMFIELD, LEONARD.   Language. New York, 1933.

133   HOCKETT, CHARLES F.   A Course in Modern Linguistics. New
      York, 1958.

Folklore

137   KRAPPE, ALEXANDER HAGGERTY.   The Science of Folk-Lore.
      London, 1930.

138 GEROULD, GORDON H. The Ballad of Tradition. New York, 1932.

139 THOMPSON, STITH. The Folktale. New York, 1946.

History of Criticism

145 SAINTSBURY, GEORGE. A History of English Criticism. Edinburgh, 1911.

> The English sections of the author's three-volume History of Criticism and Literary Taste in Europe (Edinburgh, 1900-04).

146 ATKINS, J. W. H. English Literary Criticism: The Medieval Phase. New York, 1943.

147 ———. English Literary Criticism: The Renascence. London, 1947.

148 ———. English Literary Criticism: Seventeenth and Eighteenth Centuries. London, 1951.

> For important strictures on Atkins as well as an excellent introduction to the difficulties of writing histories of criticism, see R. S. CRANE, "On Writing the History of English Criticism, 1650-1800," University of Toronto Quarterly, XXII (1952/3), 376-91.

149 ABRAMS, M. H. The Mirror and the Lamp: Romantic Theory and the Critical Tradition. New York, 1953.

150 WELLEK, RENÉ. A History of Modern Criticism: 1750-1950. New Haven, 1955- .

> To be completed in four volumes, of which the first two have been published.

151 WIMSATT, WILLIAM K., Jr., and CLEANTH BROOKS. Literary Criticism: A Short History. New York, 1957.

> Controversial. See PQ, XXXVII (1958), 307-09, and XXXVIII (1959), 299, for listing of representative reviews.

History of Poetry

157 COURTHOPE, W. J. A History of English Poetry. 6 vols. London, 1895-1910.

158 BUSH, DOUGLAS. Mythology and the Renaissance Tradition in English Poetry. Minneapolis, 1932.

> Reprinted, New York, 1957.

159   BUSH, DOUGLAS.   Mythology and the Romantic Tradition in English Poetry. Cambridge, Mass., 1937.

   Reprinted, New York, 1957.

History of Drama

166   HARBAGE, ALFRED.   Annals of English Drama, 975-1700. Philadelphia, 1940.

167   NICOLL, ALLARDYCE.   British Drama: An Historical Survey from the Beginnings to the Present Time. 4th ed. New York, 1957.

168   CHAMBERS, E. K.   The Mediaeval Stage. 2 vols. Oxford, 1903.

169   YOUNG, KARL.   The Drama of the Medieval Church. 2 vols. Oxford, 1933.

170   CRAIG, HARDIN.   English Religious Drama of the Middle Ages. Oxford, 1955.

171   CHAMBERS, E. K.   The Elizabethan Stage. 4 vols. Oxford, 1923.

   Index by Beatrice White (Oxford, 1934).

172   BENTLEY, GERALD EADES.   The Jacobean and Caroline Stage. Oxford, 1941- .

   To be completed in six volumes, of which five have appeared.

173   NICOLL, ALLARDYCE.   A History of English Drama, 1660-1900. Revised ed. 6 vols. Cambridge, 1952-59.

   Originally published under separate titles in seven volumes, 1923-46.

174   The London Stage 1660-1800: A Calendar of Plays, Entertainments & Afterpieces Together with Casts, Box-Receipts and Contemporary Comment. Carbondale, Ill., 1960- .

   To be completed in ten to twelve volumes.

History of Fiction

179   BAKER, ERNEST A.   The History of the English Novel. 10 vols. London, 1924-39.

180   ALLEN, WALTER.   The English Novel: A Short Critical History. London, 1954.

181 WATT, IAN. The Rise of the Novel: Studies in Defoe, Richardson, and Fielding. London, 1957.

182 STEVENSON, LIONEL. The English Novel: A Panorama. Boston, 1960.

AMERICAN LITERATURE: General Histories

187 SPILLER, ROBERT E., et al. Literary History of the United
States. 3 vols. New York, 1948.   (*"LHUS"*)

The "revised edition in one volume" (New York, 1953) omits
the bibliographical volume (Volume III of the 1948 edition).

188 QUINN, ARTHUR HOBSON, et al. The Literature of the American People. New York, 1951.

189 LÜDEKE, HENRY. Geschichte der amerikanischen Literatur.
Bern, 1952.

190 CUNLIFFE, MARCUS. The Literature of the United States. Revised ed. London, 1961.

AMERICAN LITERATURE: Period Histories

The Colonies and the Early Republic

197 TYLER, MOSES COIT. A History of American Literature, 1607-
1765. 2 vols. New York, 1878.

Reprinted in one volume, Ithaca, 1949.

198 ———. The Literary History of the American Revolution,
1763-1783. 2 vols. New York, 1897.

Reprinted, New York, 1957.

199 MILLER, PERRY. The New England Mind: From Colony to
Province. Cambridge, Mass., 1953.

200 ———. The New England Mind: The Seventeenth Century.
New York, 1939.

The Nineteenth Century

206 MATTHIESSEN, F. O. American Renaissance. New York, 1941.

The Twentieth Century

212 KAZIN, ALFRED. On Native Grounds: An Interpretation of Modern American Prose Literature. New York, 1942.

213 STRAUMANN, HEINRICH. American Literature in the Twentieth Century. London, 1951.

AMERICAN LITERATURE: Special Topics

Linguistics

219 KRAPP, GEORGE PHILIP. The English Language in America. 2 vols. New York, 1925.

220 MENCKEN, H. L. The American Language. 4th ed. New York, 1936. Supplements One and Two. New York, 1945, 1948.

221 FRANCIS, W. NELSON. The Structure of American English. New York, 1958.

Folklore

(139) THOMPSON, STITH. The Folktale. New York, 1946.

History of Criticism

233 FOERSTER, NORMAN. American Criticism. Boston, 1928.

234 JONES, HOWARD MUMFORD. The Theory of American Literature. Ithaca, 1948.

235 O'CONNOR, WILLIAM VAN. An Age of Criticism 1900-1950. Chicago, 1952.

History of Poetry

241 PEARCE, ROY HARVEY. The Continuity of American Poetry. Princeton, 1961.

History of Drama

247 QUINN, ARTHUR HOBSON. A History of the American Drama from the Beginning to the Civil War. New York, 1923.
Second edition, 1943.

248   QUINN, ARTHUR HOBSON. A History of the American Drama from the Civil War to the Present Day. 2 vols. New York, 1927.
Revised edition in one volume, 1936.

History of Fiction

254   QUINN, ARTHUR HOBSON. American Fiction: An Historical and Critical Survey. New York, 1936.

255   COWIE, ALEXANDER. The Rise of the American Novel. New York, 1948.

CULTURAL AND INTELLECTUAL HISTORY

European and English

263   RANDALL, JOHN HERMAN, Jr. The Making of the Modern Mind. New York, 1926.
Revised edition, 1940.

264   BRINTON, CRANE. Ideas and Men: The Story of Western Thought. New York, 1950.

265   TAYLOR, HENRY OSBORN. The Mediaeval Mind. 4th ed. 2 vols. New York, 1925.

266   CASPARI, FRITZ. Humanism and the Social Order in Tudor England. Chicago, 1954.

267   WILLEY, BASIL. The Seventeenth Century Background. London, 1934.

268   LOVEJOY, ARTHUR O. The Great Chain of Being. Cambridge, Mass., 1936.

269   BECKER, CARL L. The Heavenly City of the Eighteenth Century Philosophers. New Haven, 1932.

270   WILLEY, BASIL. The Eighteenth Century Background. London, 1940.

271   HOUGHTON, WALTER E. The Victorian Frame of Mind, 1830-1870. New Haven, 1957.

272   WHITEHEAD, ALFRED NORTH. Science and the Modern World. New York, 1925.

American

278 PARRINGTON, VERNON LOUIS. Main Currents in American Thought. 3 vols. New York, 1927-30.

(206) MATTHIESSEN, F. O. American Renaissance. New York, 1941.

279 COMMAGER, HENRY STEELE. The American Mind. New Haven, 1950.

280 CURTI, MERLE. The Growth of American Thought. 2nd ed. New York, 1951.

GUIDES TO LIBRARIES: American

General and Regional

287 DOWNS, ROBERT B. American Library Resources: A Bibliographical Guide. Chicago, 1951.

288 ASH, LEE. Subject Collections: A Guide to Special Book Collections and Subject Emphases as Reported by University, College, Public and Special Libraries in the United States and Canada. 2nd ed. New York, 1961.

  Supersedes American Library Directory Supplement, 1923-54.

289 DOWNS, ROBERT B. Resources of New York City Libraries. Chicago, 1942.

290 HILL, DAVID SPENCE. The Libraries of Washington. Chicago, 1936.

291 DOWNS, ROBERT B. Resources of Southern Libraries. Chicago, 1938.

292 VAN MALE, JOHN. Resources of Pacific Northwest Libraries. Seattle, 1943.

Individual

298 Harvard. See file of the Harvard Library Bulletin (653) and annual reports of the Houghton Library.

299 **Yale.** See file of the Yale University Library Gazette, 1926- .
(Cumulative index, Vols. I-XXXI.) See also WILMARTH S.
LEWIS, The Yale Collections (New Haven, 1946), pp. 1-13.

300 **American Antiquarian Society.** See CLARENCE S. BRIGHAM,
Fifty Years of Collecting Americana (Worcester, Mass., 1958).

301 **John Carter Brown Library.** See LAWRENCE C. WROTH, The
First Century of the John Carter Brown Library (Providence,
R.I., 1946).

302 **New York Public Library.** See KARL BROWN, A Guide to the
Reference Collections of the New York Public Library (New
York, 1941); file of the library's Bulletin (**655**); and, on the
Berg Collection, JOHN D. GORDAN, "A Doctor's Benefaction,"
PBSA, XLVIII (1954), 303-14.

303 **The Morgan Library.** See GEORGE K. BOYCE, "Modern Literary Manuscripts in the Morgan Library," *PMLA,* LXVII
(1952), No. 2, pp. 3-36; and BOYCE, "The Pierpont Morgan
Library," Library Quarterly, XXII (1952), 21-35.

304 **Library of Congress.** See DAVID C. MEARNS, "The Story up to
Now," in Annual Report of the Librarian of Congress for the
Fiscal Year Ending June 30, 1946 (Washington, 1947), pp. 13-
227; thenceforth the annual reports of the Librarian, and the
library's Quarterly Journal of Current Acquisitions, especially
the reports of the manuscript and rare book divisions.

305 **The Folger Library.** See JOSEPH QUINCY ADAMS, The Folger
Shakespeare Memorial Library (Washington, 1942); JAMES
G. McMANAWAY, "The Folger Shakespeare Library," Shake-
speare Survey 1 (1948), 57-78; and [LOUIS B. WRIGHT,] The
Folger Library: A Decade of Growth 1950-1960 (Washington,
1960).

306 **Newberry Library.** See SPARGO (**14**), 2nd edition, items 91-
100.

307 **University of Texas Library.** See file of the Library Chronicle of the University of Texas (1944-).

308 **Huntington Library.** See surveys of holdings in Huntington Library Bulletin, No. 1 (1931), 33-104, and Huntington Library Quarterly, III (1939), 131-45; and GODFREY DAVIES, "The Huntington Library," Shakespeare Survey 6 (1953), 53-63.

Catalogues

313 A Catalog of Books Represented by Library of Congress Printed Cards Issued to July 31, 1942. 167 vols. Ann Arbor, 1942-46. ("LC Catalog")
    Continued as follows:

314 Supplement: Cards Issued August 1, 1942-December 31, 1947. 42 vols. Ann Arbor, 1948.

315 The Library of Congress Author Catalog [1948-52]. 24 vols. Ann Arbor, 1953.

316 The National Union Catalog: A Cumulative Author List. Ann Arbor (later Washington), 1953- .

Many American libraries issued printed catalogues in the nineteenth century; these are often useful for bibliographical information as well as for locating copies. In addition, there are many valuable catalogues of special collections in public, college, and university libraries. For these, see DOWNS, American Library Resources (**287**).

Microfilms

322 Union List of Microfilms. Revised ed. Ann Arbor, 1951. Cumulation [of Supplements] 1949-1959. 2 vols. Ann Arbor, 1961.

GUIDES TO LIBRARIES: British

General

328 ASLIB Directory: A Guide to Sources of Information in Great Britain and Ireland, ed. Miriam Alman. 2 vols. London, 1957.
    Replaces the ASLIB Directory (London, 1928).

329 RYE, REGINALD ARTHUR. The Students' Guide to the Libraries of London. 3rd ed. London, 1927.

330 IRWIN, RAYMOND, and RONALD STAVELY, eds. The Libraries of London. 2nd ed. London, 1961.

> Supplements but does not replace **329**.

The British Museum

335 ESDAILE, ARUNDELL. The British Museum Library: A Short History and Survey. London, 1946.

> See also *TLS*, June 17 and 24, 1955, pp. 338, 356.

336 BRITISH MUSEUM. Catalogue of Printed Books. 95 vols. London, 1881-1900. Supplement. 15 vols. London, 1900-05.

> Reprinted in fifty-eight volumes, Ann Arbor, 1946. (Supplement, 10 vols., Ann Arbor, 1950.) On the many peculiarities of the cataloguing system, see Rules for Compiling the Catalogues in the Department of Printed Books in the British Museum (2nd ed., London, 1936).
> Being superseded by **337–338**.

337 ———. General Catalogue of Printed Books. 51 vols. (A-DEZW) London, 1931-54.

> Being continued by **338**.

338 ———. General Catalogue of Printed Books. Photolithographic Edition to 1955. London, 1960-   .

> To be completed in about three hundred volumes.

339 FRANCIS, F. C. "The Catalogues of the British Museum. 1. Printed Books." Journal of Documentation, IV (1948), 14-40.

340 SKEAT, T. C. "The Catalogues of the British Museum. 2. Manuscripts." Journal of Documentation, VII (1951), 18-60.

The London Library

345 Catalogue of the London Library. 2 vols. London, 1913-14. Supplements, 1913-50. 3 vols. London, 1920-53.

The John Rylands Library

351 [DUFF, E. GORDON.] Catalogue of the Printed Books and Manuscripts in the John Rylands Library. 3 vols. Manchester, 1899.

University Libraries

357 NEWCOMBE, LUXMOORE. The University and College Libraries of Great Britain and Ireland. London, 1927.

358 MUNBY, A. N. L. Cambridge College Libraries: Aids for Research Students. Cambridge, 1960.

A series of authoritative articles on great British libraries appeared in *TLS*, as follows: National Library of Wales (July 10, 1953, p. 452); National Library of Scotland (August 28, 1953, p. 555, and July 6, 1956, p. 416); Cambridge University Library (March 26, 1954, p. 207); the Bodleian Library (September 24, 1954, p. 616); Trinity College, Dublin (March 16, 1956, p. 172).

GUIDES TO LIBRARIES: Continental

La Bibliothèque Nationale

363 Catalogue générale des livres imprimés de la Bibliothèque nationale: Auteurs. Paris, 1897- .

187 volumes (A-THOM) issued to 1962.

For useful information on research libraries in various European countries, see MARGARET BURTON, Famous Libraries of
364
365 the World (London, 1937); and ARUNDELL ESDAILE and F. J. HILL, National Libraries of the World (2nd ed., London, 1957).

BIBLIOGRAPHIES OF LITERATURE: English

General

371 LOWNDES, WILLIAM T. The Bibliographer's Manual of English Literature. New ed. by Henry G. Bohn. 6 vols. London, 1857-64.

372 NORTHUP, CLARK SUTHERLAND. A Register of Bibliographies of the English Language and Literature. New Haven, 1925.

Reprinted, New York, 1962.

373   Supplemented by NATHAN VAN PATTEN, An Index to Bibliographies and Bibliographical Contributions Relating to the Work of American and British Authors, 1923-1932 (Stanford, 1934).

374   The Cambridge Bibliography of English Literature, ed. F. W. Bateson. 4 vols. Cambridge, 1941. Volume V (Supplement), ed. George Watson. Cambridge, 1957.   (*"CBEL"*)

Periods

379   ZESMER, DAVID M.   Guide to English Literature from Beowulf through Chaucer and Medieval Drama. New York, 1961.

380   HEUSINKVELD, ARTHUR H., and EDWIN J. BASHE.   A Bibliographical Guide to Old English: A Selective Bibliography of the Language, Literature, and History of the Anglo-Saxons. (University of Iowa Humanistic Studies, IV, No. 5.) Iowa City, 1931.

> See also BONSER (923).

381   WELLS, JOHN E.   A Manual of the Writings in Middle English, 1050-1400. New Haven, 1916. Supplements. 9 vols. New Haven, 1919-52.

382   TUCKER, LENA L., and ALLEN R. BENHAM.   A Bibliography of Fifteenth Century Literature. (University of Washington Publications in Language and Literature, II, No. 3.) Seattle, 1928.

383   HAZLITT, W. CAREW.   Hand-Book to the Popular, Poetical, and Dramatic Literature of Great Britain. London, 1867.

> Followed by various supplementary volumes, 1876-1903. The contents of most of these volumes are indexed in G. J. GRAY, A General Index to Hazlitt's Handbook and His Bibliographical Collections (London, 1893).

384   TOBIN, JAMES E.   Eighteenth Century English Literature and Its Cultural Background: A Bibliography. New York, 1939.

385   MILLETT, FRED B.   Contemporary British Literature. A Critical Survey and 232 Author-Bibliographies. 3rd ed. New York, 1935.

> See also DAICHES (124).

All the foregoing must be supplemented by the appropriate serial bibliographies; see below, **452-490.** For convenient summaries of recent scholarship in the various periods, see

386 LEWIS LEARY, ed., Contemporary Literary Scholarship: A Critical Review (New York, 1958), Chapters 3-10.

Types

(A) POETRY

398 BROWN, CARLETON. A Register of Middle English Religious and Didactic Verse. 2 vols. Oxford, 1916-20.

Volume II is superseded by the following item.

399 BROWN, CARLETON, and ROSSELL HOPE ROBBINS. The Index of Middle English Verse. New York, 1943.

Supplemented by WILLIAM RINGLER, *PBSA*, XLIX (1955), 153-80.

400 RAYSOR, THOMAS M. The English Romantic Poets. A Review of Research. Revised ed. New York, 1956.

401 HOUTCHENS, CAROLYN WASHBURN, and LAWRENCE HUSTON HOUTCHENS. The English Romantic Poets and Essayists: A Review of Research and Criticism. New York, 1957.

402 FAVERTY, FREDERIC E. The Victorian Poets: A Guide to Research. Cambridge, Mass., 1956.

403 KUNTZ, JOSEPH M. Poetry Explication: A Checklist of Interpretation since 1925 of British and American Poems Past and Present. Revised ed. Denver, 1962.

Supplemented by annual check lists of explications, printed
404 in The Explicator.

Cumulative index, Volumes I-XX.

(B) DRAMA

410 STRATMAN, CARL J. Bibliography of Medieval Drama. Berkeley, 1954.

411 GREG, W. W. A Bibliography of the English Printed Drama to the Restoration. 4 vols. London, 1939-59.

412 WOODWARD, GERTRUDE L., and JAMES G. MCMANAWAY. A
     Check List of English Plays 1641-1700. Chicago, 1945.
       Supplement by Fredson Bowers (Charlottesville, Va., 1949).

413 BAKER, BLANCH M. Theatre and Allied Arts: A Guide to
     Books Dealing with the History, Criticism, and Technic of the
     Drama and Theatre and Related Arts and Crafts. New York,
     1952.

A wealth of bibliographical material concerning the English
drama is also found in the standard histories and reference
works mentioned above: YOUNG (169), CHAMBERS (168, 171),
BENTLEY (172), and NICOLL (173).

(c) FICTION

419 O'DELL, STERG. A Chronological List of Prose Fiction in Eng-
     lish Printed in England and Other Countries 1475-1640. Cam-
     bridge, Mass., 1954.

420 MISH, CHARLES C. English Prose Fiction, 1600-1700. 3 vols.
     Charlottesville, Va., 1952.

421 MCBURNEY, WILLIAM HARLIN. A Check List of English Prose
     Fiction 1700-39. Cambridge, Mass., 1960.

422 BLOCK, ANDREW. The English Novel, 1740-1850. A Catalogue
     Including Prose Romances, Short Stories, and Translations of
     Foreign Fiction. London, 1939.
       Incomplete and unreliable. See *TLS*, March 25, 1939, p. 180.
       New edition, London, 1961; see *TLS*, April 21, 1961, p. 256.

423 SADLEIR, MICHAEL. Nineteenth Century Fiction: A Biblio-
     graphical Record Based on His Own Collection. 2 vols. Cam-
     bridge, 1951.

424 BELL, INGLIS F., and DONALD BAIRD. The English Novel, 1578-
     1956: A Checklist of Twentieth-Century Criticisms. Denver,
     1958.

425 THURSTON, JARVIS, et al. Short Fiction Criticism: A Checklist
     of Interpretation since 1925 of Stories and Novelettes (Amer-
     ican, British, Continental) 1800-1958. Denver, 1960.

426 STALLMAN, ROBERT WOOSTER. "A Selected Bibliography of Criticism of Modern Fiction," in John W. Aldridge, ed., Critiques and Essays on Modern Fiction 1920-1951 (New York, 1952), pp. 553-610.

(D) CRITICISM

427 STALLMAN, ROBERT WOOSTER. "Bibliography 1920-1950 [of critical theory]." The Critic's Notebook (Minneapolis, 1950), pp. 255-93.

428 ———. "A Selected Bibliography of Modern Criticism, 1920-1948." Critiques and Essays in Criticism (New York, 1949), pp. 519-71.

BIBLIOGRAPHIES OF LITERATURE: American

General

429 [JOHNSON, THOMAS H., ed.] Bibliography. Vol. III of SPILLER, Literary History of the United States (187). Supplement, ed. Richard M. Ludwig. New York, 1959.

430 BLANCK, JACOB. Bibliography of American Literature. New Haven, 1955- .

Three volumes (HENRY ADAMS–BRET HARTE) have appeared.

431 STOVALL, FLOYD. Eight American Authors: A Review of Research and Criticism. New York, 1956.

432 MILLETT, FRED B. Contemporary American Authors: A Critical Survey and 219 Bio-Bibliographies. New York, 1940.

433 LEARY, LEWIS. Articles on American Literature, 1900-1950. Durham, N.C., 1954.

434 GOHDES, CLARENCE. Bibliographical Guide to the Study of the Literature of the U. S. A. Durham, N.C., 1959.

435 JONES, HOWARD MUMFORD. Guide to American Literature and Its Backgrounds since 1890. 2nd ed. Cambridge, Mass., 1959.

Types

(A) DRAMA

439 See MONTROSE J. MOSES, Representative American Dramas (2nd ed., New York, 1933), pp. 865-90, and QUINN (**247, 248**).

(B) FICTION

445 WRIGHT, LYLE H. American Fiction 1774-1850: A Contribution toward a Bibliography. Revised ed. San Marino, Cal., 1948.

446 Continued by the same author's American Fiction: 1851-1875 (San Marino, 1957).

447 GERSTENBERGER, DONNA, and GEORGE HENDRICK. The American Novel 1789-1959: A Checklist of Twentieth-Century Criticism. Denver, 1961.

See also JARVIS THURSTON et al., Short Fiction Criticism (**425**).

(C) CRITICISM
See STALLMAN (**427, 428**).

For summaries of recent scholarship in American literature, see LEARY, Contemporary Literary Scholarship (**386**), Chapters 12-15.

SERIAL BIBLIOGRAPHIES OF LITERATURE

General

452 MODERN HUMANITIES RESEARCH ASSOCIATION. Annual Bibliography of English Language and Literature [1920-   ]. Cambridge, 1921-   .   ("MHRA Bibliography")

453 "Annual Bibliography [1921-   ]." *PMLA*, 1922-   .
                                        (*"PMLA* Bibliography")
Previous to issue for 1956, included books and articles by American scholars only.

454 ENGLISH ASSOCIATION. The Year's Work in English Studies
[1919-]. London, 1921- .   (*"YWES"*)

English: Periods

460 "Literature of the Renaissance." Annually in *SP*, 1917- .

461 On Shakespeare and related topics, see also "Shakespeare:
An Annotated Bibliography [1949-]," annually in Shake-
462 speare Quarterly, 1950- , and "The Year's Contributions to
Shakespearian Study" in Shakespeare Survey, 1948- .

463 "English Literature, 1660-1800: A Current Bibliography
[1925-]." Annually in *PQ*, 1926- .

464 Issues for 1925-60 collected in LOUIS A. LANDA et al., English Literature, 1660-1800: A Bibliography of Modern Studies
(4 vols., Princeton, 1950-52, 1962).

465 "The Romantic Movement: A Selective and Critical Bibliography [1936-]." Annually in *ELH*, 1937-49, and *PQ*, 1950- .

466 See also "Current Bibliography [of Keats, Shelley, Byron,
Hunt, etc., 1950-]." Annually in Keats-Shelley Journal,
1952- .

467 "Victorian Bibliography [1932-]." Annually in *MP*, 1933-
57, and Victorian Studies, 1958- .

468 Issues for 1932-54 collected in WILLIAM D. TEMPLEMAN,
Bibliographies of Studies in Victorian Literature for . . .
469 1932-1944 (Urbana, Ill., 1945) and AUSTIN WRIGHT,
Bibliographies of Studies in Victorian Literature for . . .
1945-1954 (Urbana, Ill., 1956).

470 "Current Bibliography [of Twentieth-Century Literature,
1954-]." Quarterly in Twentieth-Century Literature: A
Scholarly and Critical Journal, 1955- .

American

471 "Articles on American Literature Appearing in Current Periodicals [1929-]." Quarterly in *AL*, 1929- .

All materials appearing in this bibliography through 1950 are
gathered in LEARY, Articles on American Literature, 1900-1950
(**433**).

472 "Articles in American Studies [1954-]." Annually in American Quarterly, 1955- .

Special Topics

478 "A Bibliography of Critical Arthurian Literature [1936-]." Annually in *MLQ*, 1940- .

479 Preceded by JOHN J. PARRY and MARGARET SCHLAUCH, A Bibliography of Critical Arthurian Literature for the Years 1922-29 (New York, 1931), and Volume II of the same (for
480 1930-35) (New York, 1936). See also Bulletin bibliographique de la Société internationale arthurienne, 1949- .

481 "A Selective Check List of Bibliographical Scholarship [1949-]." Annually in Studies in Bibliography, 1950/1- .
Issues for 1949-55 gathered, with full index, in Studies in Bibliography, X (1957).

482 "Annual Bibliography [of Comparative Literature, 1949-]." Annually in Yearbook of Comparative and General Literature, 1952- .

483 An annual supplement to FERNAND BALDENSPERGER and WERNER P. FRIEDRICH, Bibliography of Comparative Literature (Chapel Hill, N.C., 1950).

484 Bibliographie générale de littérature comparée [1949-]. Paris, 1950- .

485 "Anglo-German Literary Bibliography [1933-]." Annually in *JEGP*, 1935- .

486 "Selective Current Bibliography for Aesthetics and Related Fields [1945-]." Annually in Journal of Aesthetics and Art Criticism, 1945/6- .

487 "Annual Bibliography of Folklore [1887-]." Journal of American Folklore, 1888- .

488 "Folklore Bibliography [1937-]." Southern Folklore Quarterly, 1938- .

489 "Modern Drama: A Selective Bibliography of Works Published in English in [1959-]." Annually in Modern Drama, 1960- .

490 An Index to Book Reviews in the Humanities. Detroit, 1960- .

GENERAL REFERENCE GUIDES

494 MALCLÈS, LOUISE-NOËLLE. Les Sources du travail bibliographique. 3 vols. in 4. Geneva, 1950-58.

495 WINCHELL, CONSTANCE M. Guide to Reference Books. 7th ed. Chicago, 1951. Supplements, 1950-58. 3 vols. Chicago, 1954-60.

496 SHORES, LOUIS. Basic Reference Sources: An Introduction to Materials and Methods. Chicago, 1954.

497 WALFORD, A. J. Guide to Reference Material. London, 1959.

BIBLIOGRAPHIES OF BIBLIOGRAPHIES

502 BESTERMAN, THEODORE. A World Bibliography of Bibliographies. 3rd ed. 4 vols. Geneva, 1955-56.

503 COURTNEY, WILLIAM P. A Register of National Bibliography. 3 vols. London, 1905-12.

504 Bibliographic Index: A Cumulative Bibliography of Bibliographies [1937-]. New York, 1938- .

505 On books of this class, as well as of the three following classes, see ROBERT L. COLLISON, Bibliographies: Subject and National (New York, 1951).

UNIVERSAL BIBLIOGRAPHIES

511 WATT, ROBERT. Bibliotheca Britannica; or a General Index to British and Foreign Literature. 4 vols. Edinburgh, 1824.

512 GRÄSSE, JOHANN GEORG THEODOR. Trésor de livres rares et précieux. 7 vols. Dresden, 1859-69.

513 BRUNET, JACQUES CHARLES. Manuel du libraire et de l'amateur de livres. 6 vols. Paris, 1860-65. Supplement. 2 vols. Paris, 1878-80.

Additional volume (1870): Dictionnaire de géographie ancienne et moderne.

AUTHOR BIBLIOGRAPHIES

See WINCHELL (495) and WALFORD (497), as well as many of the items listed under Bibliographies of Literature and Serial Bibliographies of Literature.

SUBJECT CATALOGUES

519 Subject Index of the Modern Works Added to the Library of the British Museum [1881-]. London, 1902- .

("Fortescue," after its first editor.)

520 Subject-Index of the London Library. 4 vols. London, 1909-55.

521 PEDDIE, R. A. Subject Index of Books Published before 1880. 4 vols. London, 1933-48.

522 Library of Congress Catalog: Books: Subjects [1950-]. Ann Arbor, 1955; Washington, 1956- .

523 Subject Guide to Books in Print. New York, 1957- .

For the work to which this is a subject-index, see Publishers' Trade List Annual (813).

For further subject-indexing, see the British Museum General Catalogue (336-338) (for authors as subjects), the printed catalogues of individual American and British libraries, the Cumulative Book Index (811), the American Book Publishing Record (815), the Reference Catalogue of Current Literature (790), the English Catalogue (787), Whitaker's Cumulative Booklist (788), and the British National Bibliography (789). For subject-indexing of periodicals, see 680-687. See also the indexes to the Bulletin of the New York Public Library (655), a periodical which often prints valuable subject bibliographies.

INDEXES TO COMPOSITE BOOKS

529 The "A.L.A." Index: An Index to General Literature. 2nd ed. Boston, 1901. Supplement, 1900-10. Chicago, 1914.

530 Essay and General Literature Index, 1900-33. New York, 1934. Supplementary volumes. New York, 1941- .

GUIDES TO ANONYMOUS AND PSEUDONYMOUS LITERATURE

536 HALKETT, SAMUEL, and JOHN LAING. Dictionary of Anonymous and Pseudonymous English Literature. New ed. 9 vols. Edinburgh, 1926-62.

> For further help in identifying the authors of anonymous and pseudonymous works, see ARCHER TAYLOR and FREDERIC J. MOSHER, The Bibliographical History of Anonyma and Pseudonyma (Chicago, 1951).

The Supplement to the LC Catalog (314) identifies the authors of "approximately 26,000 anonymous and pseudonymous" works.

GENERAL ENCYCLOPEDIAS

542 Encyclopaedia Britannica. 11th ed. 29 vols. New York, 1910-11.

> Later editions are less useful for scholarly purposes.

543 Enciclopedia Italiana. 35 vols. and index. Rome, 1929-39. Supplements 1 and 2. Rome, 1938, 1948-49.

544 La Grande Encyclopédie. 31 vols. Paris, 1886-1902.

545 The Catholic Encyclopedia. 16 vols. New York, 1907-14. Supplements 1 and 2. New York, 1922, 1951.

546 The Century Dictionary and Cyclopedia. 12 vols. New York, 1911.

> A new edition of the Cyclopedia of Names was published in 1954.

547 Encyclopaedia of Religion and Ethics, ed. James Hastings. 13 vols. New York, 1908-27.

548 Encyclopaedia of the Social Sciences, ed. Edwin R. A. Seligman and Alvin Johnson. 15 vols. New York, 1930-35.

549 Grove's Dictionary of Music and Musicians, ed. Eric Blom. 5th ed. 9 vols. London, 1954. Supplementary volume. London, 1961.

550 The Jewish Encyclopedia. 12 vols. New York, 1901-06.

551 Dictionary of Philosophy and Psychology, ed. James Mark Baldwin. 3 vols. New York, 1901-05.

Reprinted 1940-49. Volume III is an important bibliography of individual philosophers and general topics.

For comments on these encyclopedias, as well as the titles of numerous others in various fields of interest, see WINCHELL (495) and WALFORD (497).

DICTIONARIES

English

557 A New English Dictionary on Historical Principles, ed. James A. H. Murray et al. 10 vols. in 15. Oxford, 1888-1928.

(*"NED"* or *"OED"*)

The "corrected reissue," with supplement, is called The Oxford English Dictionary (13 vols., Oxford, 1933).

558 The Shorter Oxford English Dictionary, ed. William Little et al. 3rd ed. Oxford, 1955.

559 FOWLER, H. W. A Dictionary of Modern English Usage. London, 1926.

Reprinted 1937. Cf. NICHOLSON (568).

560 PARTRIDGE, ERIC. A Dictionary of Slang and Unconventional English. 5th ed. 2 vols. London, 1961.

American

566 A Dictionary of American English on Historical Principles, ed. William Craigie and James R. Hulbert. 4 vols. Chicago, 1938-44. (*"DAE"*)

567 A Dictionary of Americanisms, ed. Mitford M. Mathews. 2 vols. Chicago, 1951.

568 NICHOLSON, MARGARET. A Dictionary of American-English Usage. New York, 1957.

> Based on FOWLER (559).

569 WENTWORTH, HAROLD, and STUART BERG FLEXNER. Dictionary of American Slang. New York, 1960.

Greek

574 A Greek-English Lexicon, ed. Henry George Liddell et al. Revised ed. 10 parts in 2 vols. Oxford, 1925-40.

Latin

580 Harper's Latin Dictionary, ed. E. A. Andrews. Revised ed. New York, 1907.

> "Founded on the translation of Freund's Latin-German Lexicon."

581 Cassell's New Latin-English, English-Latin Dictionary, ed. D. P. Simpson. London, 1959.

French

587 Heath's Standard French and English Dictionary, ed. J. E. Mansion. 2 vols. Boston, 1934-39.

> Reprinted with corrections, Boston, 1956. English title: Harrap's Standard French and English Dictionary.

588 The New Cassell's French Dictionary, ed. Denis Girard et al. New York, 1962.

German

594 Encyclopaedic English-German and German-English Dictionary, ed. Eduard Muret, Daniel Sanders, et al. 2 vols. in 4. Berlin, 1900-01.

595 Cassell's German and English Dictionary, ed. Harold T. Betteridge. London, 1957.

Spanish

601 A New Pronouncing Dictionary of the Spanish and English Languages, ed. Mariano Velázquez de la Cadena. Revised ed. 2 vols. New York, 1900-02.

602 Cassell's Spanish Dictionary: Spanish-English, English-Spanish, ed. Allison Peers et al. London, 1959.

SCHOLARLY PERIODICALS

A list limited to journals most often consulted by scholars in English and American literature. For the full range of periodicals that have some bearing on literary studies, see the long list prefixed to the *PMLA* Annual Bibliography (453). See also

607 "American Journals in the Humanities: A Guide to Scope and Editorial Policy," *PMLA*, LXXII (1957), No. 4, Part 2, pp.

608 52-65; MILTON BRUCE BYRD and ARNOLD L. GOLDSMITH, Publication Guide for Literary and Linguistic Scholars (Wayne State University Studies, Humanities, No. 4, Detroit, 1958);

609 and DONNA GERSTENBERGER and GEORGE HENDRICK, Directory of Periodicals Publishing Articles in English and American Language and Literature (Denver, 1959).

English and American Literature Exclusively

614 Abstracts of English Studies. 1958- .

615 American Literature. 1929/30- . ("*AL*")
    Cumulative index, Volumes I-XX.

616 Anglia. 1877- .
    Cumulative indexes to Volumes I-L, LI-LXXV.

617 ELH. 1934- .

618 Englische Studien. 1877-1944.
    Cumulative indexes to Volumes I-XXIII, XXIV-XXV, XXVI-L.

619 English Institute Essays. 1939- .
    Title, 1939-42: English Institute Annual. Volumes published under individual titles, 1953 onward.

620 English Studies [Amsterdam]. 1919- .
    Cumulative index, Volumes I-XL.

620a Etudes Anglaises. 1937- .

621 Keats-Shelley Journal. 1952- .

622 Nineteenth Century Fiction. 1945- .
Title, 1945-49: The Trollopian.

622a A Review of English Literature. 1960- .

623 Review of English Studies. 1925- .   (*"RES"*)
See F. W. BATESON, "Organs of Critical Opinion. I: The Review of English Studies," Essays in Criticism, VI (1956), 190-201.

624 Shakespeare Quarterly. 1950- .

625 Shakespeare Survey. 1948- .
Published annually. Cumulative index, Volumes I-X, in Volume X.

626 Studies in English Literature 1500-1900. 1961- .

In addition, there are many informal organs of specialized groups which contain useful notes, articles, reviews, etc.; for example, the Shakespeare Newsletter, Renaissance News, the Seventeenth-Century News, Johnsonian News Letter, the Victorian Newsletter, the Thoreau Society Bulletin, the Walt Whitman Review.

Modern Languages and Literatures
(Including English and American)

631 Journal of English and Germanic Philology. 1897- .
                                                        (*"JEGP"*)

632 PMLA: Publications of the Modern Language Association of America. 1884/5- .
Cumulative indexes to Volumes I-L, LI-LX.

633 Modern Language Notes. 1886- .   (*"MLN"*)
Cumulative indexes to Volumes I-L, LI-LX.
Beginning in 1962, limited to Romance and German languages and literatures.

634 Modern Language Quarterly. 1940- .   (*"MLQ"*)

635 Modern Language Review. 1905/6- .   (*"MLR"*)
Cumulative indexes to Volumes I-X, XI-XX, XXI-L.

636 Modern Philology. 1903/4- .   (*"MP"*)

637 Philological Quarterly. 1922- .   *("PQ")*

Cumulative index to Volumes I-XXV.

638 Studies in Philology. 1906- .   *("SP")*

Cumulative index to Volumes I-L.

Analytical Bibliography, History of Printing, etc.

645 The Library. 1889- .

Merged in 1920 with the Transactions of the Bibliographical Society, begun in 1893.

Indexed in GEORGE W. COLE, An Index to Bibliographical Papers Published by the Bibliographical Society and the Library Association, London, 1877-1932 (Chicago, 1933).

646 Papers of the Bibliographical Society of America. 1904/5- .

("PBSA")

Cumulative indexes to Volumes I-XXV, XXVI-XLV.

647 Studies in Bibliography. Papers of the Bibliographical Society of the University of Virginia. 1948/9- .

Published annually.

Publications of Research Libraries

653 Harvard Library Bulletin. 1947-60.

Cumulative indexes to Volumes I-X, XI-XIV.

654 Huntington Library Quarterly. 1937/8- .

Preceded by Huntington Library Bulletin, 1931-37.

655 Bulletin of the New York Public Library. 1897- .

Cumulative index to Volumes I-XL.

Allied Fields

661 American Speech. 1925/6- .

662 Comparative Literature. 1949- .

Cumulative index to Volumes I-X.

663 Journal of Aesthetics and Art Criticism. 1941- .

664 The Journal of American Folklore. 1888- .

Cumulative index to Volumes I-LXX.

665 Journal of the History of Ideas. 1940- .   (*"JHI"*)

666 New England Quarterly. 1928- .
Cumulative index to Volumes I-X.

667 Speculum. 1926- .

668 Studies in Romanticism. 1961- .
Preceded by Boston University Studies in English, 1955-61.

669 Victorian Studies. 1957- .

Little Magazines

See HOFFMAN, The Little Magazine (**720**).

General

673 The [London] Times Literary Supplement. 1902- . (*"TLS"*)
See Fiftieth Anniversary Number, January 18, 1952; and F. W. BATESON, "Organs of Critical Opinion. IV: The Times Literary Supplement," Essays in Criticism, VII (1957), 349-62, and ensuing correspondence in *TLS*. See also MILTON MAYER, "Friend, This is the Times Literary Supplement," Esquire, LII (November 1959), 125-29.

674 Notes and Queries. 1849/50- .   (*"N&Q"*)
Fifteen cumulative indexes through 1947.

675 American Notes & Queries. 1962- .

GENERAL PERIODICALS AND NEWSPAPERS

Indexes to Periodicals

680 Poole's Index to Periodical Literature, 1802-81. Revised ed. Boston, 1891. Supplements, 1882-1907. 5 vols. Boston, 1887-1908.
Use with MARION V. BELL and JEAN C. BACON, Poole's Index Date and Volume Key (Chicago, 1957), which supersedes the "Chronological Conspectus" of the original Poole volumes.

681 Nineteenth Century Readers' Guide to Periodical Literature, 1890-99. 2 vols. New York, 1944.

682 The Magazine Subject-Index: A Subject-Index to Seventy-Nine American and English Periodicals. 2 vols. Boston, 1908.

[*Continued*]

683 Continued by Annual Magazine Subject-Index [1909-49] (Boston, 1910-52).

684 Readers' Guide to Periodical Literature [1900-]. Minneapolis (later New York), 1901- .

685 International Index to Periodicals [1907-]. New York, 1916- .
First two volumes titled Readers' Guide to Periodical Literature Supplement.

686 British Humanities Index. 1962- .
A continuation, with altered scope, of the Subject Index to Periodicals (London, 1916-61).

687 Index to Little Magazines [1948-]. Denver, 1949- .

Indexes to Newspapers

693 The New York Times Index [1913-]. New York, 1913- .
In addition, nearly complete indexes, 1851-1905, are available on microfilm.

694 Palmer's Index to the [London] Times Newspaper [1790-1941]. London, 1868-1943.

695 The [London] Times. Official Index [1906-]. London, 1907- .

Bibliographies and Location Guides

702 Union List of Serials in Libraries of the United States and Canada, ed. Winifred Gregory. 2nd ed. New York, 1943. Supplements, 1941-49. 2 vols. New York, 1945-53.
("Gregory," "*ULS*")

703 Supplemented by New Serial Titles (Washington, 1950-).

For a bibliography of printed union lists of serials for various geographical regions, cities, etc., see the main volume of Gregory, pp. 3053-65.

704 British Union-Catalogue of Periodicals. 4 vols. London, 1955-58. Supplement. London, 1962.

705 Union Catalogue of the Periodical Publications in the University Libraries of the British Isles, ed. Marion G. Roupell. London, 1937.

706 BRITISH MUSEUM. Periodical Publications. 2nd ed. London, 1899-1900.

(Volume XLI in the Ann Arbor reprint of the British Museum Catalogue of Printed Books [**336**].)

707 [MUDDIMAN, J. G.] The Times Tercentenary Handlist of English and Welsh Newspapers, Magazines and Reviews [1620-1920]. London, 1920.

To be used with caution. See corrections in *N&Q*, 1921-22.

708 BRITISH MUSEUM. Newspapers Published in Great Britain and Ireland, 1801-1900. London, 1905.

This volume of the Supplement to the British Museum Catalogue (**336**) is omitted from the Ann Arbor reprint.

709 BRIGHAM, CLARENCE S. History and Bibliography of American Newspapers 1690-1820. 2 vols. Worcester, Mass., 1947.

Additions and corrections in Proceedings of the American Antiquarian Society, LXXI (1961), 15-62.

710 American Newspapers 1821-1936: A Union List of Files Available in the United States and Canada, ed. Winifred Gregory. New York, 1937.

711 CRANE, RONALD S., and F. B. KAYE. A Census of British Newspapers and Periodicals 1620-1800. Chapel Hill, N.C., 1927. Originally published in *SP*, XXIV (1927), 1-205.

Supplemented by:

712 GABLER, ANTHONY J. "Check-List of English Newspapers and Periodicals before 1801 in the Huntington Library." Huntington Library Bulletin, No. 2 (1931), 1-66.

713 MILFORD, R. T., and D. M. SUTHERLAND. A Catalogue of English Newspapers and Periodicals in the Bodleian Library, 1622-1800. Oxford Bibliographical Society Proceedings and Papers, IV (1934/5), 163-346.

714 STEWART, POWELL. British Newspapers and Periodicals 1632-1800 [in the University of Texas Library]. Austin, 1950.

715   CRANFIELD, G. A.   A Hand-List of English Provincial Newspapers and Periodicals 1700-1760. Cambridge Bibliographical Society Monograph No. 2 (1952).

> Additions in *Transactions of the Cambridge Bibliographical
> Society*, II, Part 3 (1956), 269-74, and Part 5 (1959), 385-89.

716   WARD, WILLIAM S.   Index and Finding List of Serials Published in the British Isles, 1789-1832. Lexington, Ky., 1953.

717   WEED, KATHERINE KIRTLEY, and RICHMOND P. BOND.   Studies
of British Newspapers and Periodicals from Their Beginning
to 1800: A Bibliography. *SP*, extra series, No. 2 (1946).

For extensive lists of British newspapers and magazines, and
studies thereof, see *CBEL* (374), II, 656-739; III, 779-846; and
V, 475-83, 678-87.

---

718   Newspapers on Microfilm. 4th ed. Washington, 1961.

719   MOTT, FRANK LUTHER.   A History of American Magazines.
New York (later Cambridge, Mass.), 1930- .

> Four volumes, covering the years 1741-1905, have appeared.

720   HOFFMAN, FREDERICK J., et al.   The Little Magazine: A History and a Bibliography. Princeton, 1946.

721   See also Union List of Little Magazines [in the libraries of
six midwestern universities] (Chicago, 1956).

Extensive files of English and American periodicals, 18th-20th
centuries, are now available in many libraries on microfilm.

AIDS FOR TRACING PARTICULAR COPIES OF BOOKS

Guides to Book Collectors

727   DE RICCI, SEYMOUR.   English Collectors of Books and Manuscripts (1530-1930). New York, 1930.

> Reprinted, Bloomington, Ind., 1960.

728   CANNON, CARL L.   American Book Collectors and Collecting.
New York, 1941.

For a list of printed catalogues of some great collections formerly in private hands see KENNEDY, Concise Bibliography (15), 3rd ed., pp. 24-27.

Bibliographies of Book-Sale Catalogues

734 BRITISH MUSEUM. List of Catalogues of English Book Sales, 1676-1900, Now in the British Museum. London, 1915.

735 McKAY, GEORGE L. American Book Auction Catalogues 1713-1934: A Union List. New York, 1937.

> Additions in the Bulletin of the New York Public Library, L (1946), 177-84; LII (1948), 401-12.

Current Book-Auction Records

741 Book-Prices Current: A Record of Prices at Which Books Have Been Sold at Auction. London, 1888- .

> Three cumulative indexes, covering the years 1887-1916.

742 Book-Auction Records: A Priced and Annotated Annual Record of London, New York and Edinburgh Book Auctions [1902-]. London, 1903- .

> Six cumulative indexes, covering the years 1902-58.

743 American Book-Prices Current. New York, 1895- .

> Seven cumulative indexes, covering the years 1916-60.

744 United States Cumulative Book Auction Records. New York, 1940-51.

ANALYTICAL BIBLIOGRAPHY

750 BOWERS, FREDSON. "Bibliography, Pure Bibliography, and Literary Studies." *PBSA*, XLVI (1952), 186-208.

751 WILSON, F. P. "Shakespeare and the 'New Bibliography.'" The Bibliographical Society 1892-1942: Studies in Retrospect (London, 1945), pp. 76-135.

752 McKERROW, RONALD B. An Introduction to Bibliography for Literary Students. Oxford, 1927.

753 BOWERS, FREDSON. Principles of Bibliographical Description. Princeton, 1949.

754 ALDIS, HARRY G.   The Printed Book. 3rd ed., revised by John Carter and Brooke Crutchley. Cambridge, 1951.

755 ESDAILE, ARUNDELL, and ROY STOKES.   A Student's Manual of Bibliography. 3rd ed. London, 1954.

756 BRIQUET, CHARLES M.   Les Filigranes [1282-1600]. 2nd ed. 4 vols. Leipzig, 1923.

757 Supplemented by W. A. CHURCHILL, Watermarks in Paper in Holland, England, France, etc., in the Seventeenth and Eighteenth Centuries (Amsterdam, 1935) and by EDWARD

758 HEAWOOD, Watermarks: Mainly of the 17th and 18th Centuries (Hilversum, 1950).

BOOK-TRADE HISTORY

English

764 PLANT, MARJORIE.   The English Book Trade: An Economic History of the Making and Sale of Books. London, 1939.

765 MUMBY, FRANK ARTHUR.   Publishing and Bookselling: A History from the Earliest Times to the Present Day. 3rd ed. London, 1954.

The bibliography in this volume is the fullest guide to the literature on English publishing and bookselling.

766 DUFF, EDWARD G.   A Century of the English Book Trade [1457-1557]. London, 1905.

Continued by:

767 DUFF, E. G., et al. Hand Lists of English Printers, 1501-1556. 4 parts. London, 1895-1913.

768 McKERROW, R. B.   A Dictionary of Printers and Booksellers in England, Scotland and Ireland . . . 1557-1640. London, 1910.

769 PLOMER, HENRY R.   A Dictionary of the Booksellers and Printers . . . in England, Scotland and Ireland from 1641 to 1667. London, 1907.

770 PLOMER, HENRY R., et al. A Dictionary of the Printers and Booksellers . . . from 1668 to 1725. London, 1922.

771 ———— et al. A Dictionary of the Printers and Booksellers . . . from 1726 to 1775. London, 1932.

See also Morrison's indexes (**796, 800**) of printers, publishers, and booksellers in *STC* and Wing.

American

777 McMURTRIE, DOUGLAS C. A History of Printing in the United States. Vol. II: Middle and South Atlantic States. New York, 1936.

> This is the only volume published. For the materials McMurtrie would have incorporated into the other volumes planned, see under his name in the index of DOWNS, American Library Resources (**287**).

778 LEHMANN-HAUPT, HELLMUT, et al. The Book in America. 2nd ed. New York, 1951.

> The original edition (1939) contains sections deleted from the later edition.

NATIONAL BIBLIOGRAPHIES: *English*

Contemporary Lists

784 ARBER, EDWARD. A Transcript of the Registers of the Company of Stationers of London, 1554-1640. 5 vols. London 1875-77; Birmingham, 1894.   ("Stationers' Register")

> Reprinted, New York, 1950.

785 [EYRE, G. E. B.] A Transcript of the Registers of the Worshipful Company of Stationers from 1640-1708. 3 vols. London, 1913-14.

> Reprinted, New York, 1950.

786 ARBER, EDWARD. The Term Catalogues, 1668-1709. A Contemporary Bibliography of English Literature in the Reigns of Charles II, James II, William and Mary, and Anne. 3 vols. London, 1903-06.

787 The English Catalogue of Books Published [1801-   ]. London, 1864-   .

> Period 1801-36 is covered in a retrospective volume, ed. Robert Alexander Peddie and Quintin Waddington (London, 1914). From 1837 onward, a contemporary list, published annually and then cumulated into larger volumes at varying intervals. Basis of the list is the weekly one appearing in British Books (the title since 1959 of the former Publishers' Circular).

788 Whitaker's Cumulative Booklist. London, 1924-   .

> Based on weekly list appearing in The Bookseller.

789 The British National Bibliography. London, 1950-   .

> Published weekly; cumulated quarterly, annually, and quinquennially.

790 The Reference Catalogue of Current Literature. London, 1874-   .

See also Cumulative Book Index (**811**).

Retrospective Lists

795 POLLARD, A. W., and G. R. REDGRAVE.   A Short-Title Catalogue of Books Printed in England, Scotland, and Ireland, and of English Books Printed Abroad, 1475-1640. London, 1926.
("STC")

796 Indexed in PAUL G. MORRISON, Index of Printers, Publishers and Booksellers in [the Short-Title Catalogue] (Charlottesville, Va., 1950).

797 See also WILLIAM WARNER BISHOP, A Checklist of American Copies of "Short-Title Catalogue" Books (2nd ed., Ann
798 Arbor, 1950), and DAVID RAMAGE, A Finding-List of English Books to 1640 in Libraries in the British Isles (Durham, 1958).

> All works listed in the STC are being made available on microfilm.

799 WING, DONALD.   Short-Title Catalogue of Books Printed in England, Scotland, Ireland, Wales, and British America and of English Books Printed in Other Countries, 1641-1700. 3 vols. New York, 1945-51.   [Continued]

800 Indexed in PAUL G. MORRISON, Index of Printers, Publishers and Booksellers [in Wing] (Charlottesville, Va., 1955).

801 See also supplement in Huntington Library Quarterly, XVI (1953), 393-436.

A large selection of the works listed in Wing is being made available on microfilm.

NATIONAL BIBLIOGRAPHIES: American

Contemporary Lists

807 ROORBACH, O. A.   Bibliotheca Americana. Catalogue of American Publications 1820-[1861]. 4 vols. New York, 1852-61.

808 The American Catalogue of Books [1861-71]. 2 vols. New York, 1866-71.

Reprinted, New York, 1938.

809 The American Catalogue of Books [1876-1910]. 13 vols. New York, 1880-1911.

Reprinted, New York, 1941.

810 United States Catalog. 4th ed.: Books in Print January 1, 1928. New York, 1928.

Earlier editions published 1899, 1902, 1912. For books, published in the intervals between these editions, which went out of print before the next edition, see appropriate volumes of the next item.

811 Cumulative Book Index [1898-   ]. Minneapolis (later New York), 1900-   .   (*"CBI"*)

Note subtitle: "*World* List of Books in English." The current supplement to the United States Catalog.

812 Publishers' Weekly. New York, 1872-   .

Weekly lists of newly published books.

813 The Publishers' Trade List Annual [1873-   ]. New York, 1874-   .

814
(523) Indexed in Books in Print: An Author-Title-Series Index to the Publishers' Trade List Annual (New York, 1948-   ) and in Subject Guide to Books in Print (New York, 1957-   ).

815 American Book Publishing Record. New York, 1960- .

Of narrower scope but of special usefulness are Paperbound Books in Print (New York, 1955-), Paperbacks in Print (London, 1960-), and Scholarly Books in America: A Quarterly Bibliography of University Press Publications (Chicago, 1959-).

Retrospective Lists

821 SABIN, JOSEPH. Bibliotheca Americana: A Dictionary of Books Relating to America, from its Discovery to the Present Time. 29 vols. New York, 1868-1936.

> For important information about the successive reductions of scope during the long process of compilation, see introduction to Volume XXIX. (Since the contents are not limited to books published in America this is not, strictly speaking, a national bibliography.)

822 EVANS, CHARLES. American Bibliography: A Chronological Dictionary of All Books, Pamphlets and Periodical Publications Printed in the United States of America from the Genesis of Printing in 1639 down to and Including the Year 1820. 13 vols. and index. Chicago (later Worcester, Mass.), 1903-59.

> Reaches only through 1800. All items listed (ca. 30,000) are now being made available in microprint.

823 Indexed in ROGER PATTRELL BRISTOL, Index of Printers, Publishers, and Booksellers [in Evans] (Charlottesville, Va., 1961).

824 SHAW, RALPH R., and RICHARD H. SHOEMAKER. American Bibliography: A Preliminary Checklist [1801-19]. New York, 1958- .

> Volumes for 1801-10 have so far been issued.

NATIONAL BIBLIOGRAPHIES: Other Nations

For annotated lists of the older and currently appearing national bibliographies of European and South American countries, see WINCHELL (495), MALCLÈS (494), and HELEN F.

828 CONOVER, Current National Bibliographies (Washington, 1955).

GUIDES TO DISSERTATIONS

834 PALFREY, THOMAS R., and HENRY E. COLEMAN, Jr. Guide to Bibliographies of Theses, United States and Canada. 2nd ed. Chicago, 1940.

Additions in Bulletin of Bibliography, XVIII (1945), 181-82, 201-03.

835 LIBRARY OF CONGRESS. A List of American Doctoral Dissertations Printed in [1912-38]. Washington, 1913-40.

836 Doctoral Dissertations Accepted by American Universities [1933/4-1954/5]. New York, 1934-55.

Beginning with 1955/6, combined with Index to American Doctoral Dissertations (in 837).

837 Dissertation Abstracts. Ann Arbor, 1938- .

Title, 1938-51: Microfilm Abstracts.
Cumulative index to Volumes I-XI (1938-51).

838 WOODRESS, JAMES. Dissertations in American Literature, 1891-1955, with Supplement 1956-1961. Durham, N.C., 1962.

Continued by list of completed dissertations in each issue of American Literature (615), which also contains a record of dissertations in progress.

839 MUMMENDEY, RICHARD. Language and Literature of the Anglo-Saxon Nations as Presented in German Doctoral Dissertations 1885-1950. Charlottesville, Va., 1954.

Seriously incomplete.

840 Index to Theses Accepted for Higher Degrees in the Universities of Great Britain and Ireland [1950/1-]. London, 1953- .

841 ALTICK, RICHARD D., and WILLIAM R. MATTHEWS. Guide to Dissertations in Victorian Literature 1886-1958. Urbana, Ill., 1960.

MANUSCRIPTS

Catalogues of Manuscripts

850 RICHARDSON, ERNEST CUSHING. A List of Printed Catalogs of Manuscript Books. (Part III of A Union World Catalog of Manuscript Books.) New York, 1935.

"Indispensable but uncritical and full of errors" (Paul Kristeller).

851 KRISTELLER, PAUL OSKAR. Latin Manuscript Books Before 1600: A List of the Printed Catalogues and Unpublished Inventories of Extant Collections. New York, 1960.

Has broader usefulness than the title indicates.

852 BRITISH MUSEUM. Catalogue of Additions to the Manuscripts in the British Museum. London, 1901- .

Eight volumes (covering the years 1894-1930) published to 1959.

(340) SKEAT, T. C. "The Catalogues of the British Museum. 2. Manuscripts." Journal of Documentation, VII (1951), 18-60.

853 HUNT, R. W., et al. A Summary Catalogue of Western Manuscripts in the Bodleian Library at Oxford. 7 vols. in 8. Oxford, 1895-1953.

854 HISTORICAL MANUSCRIPTS COMMISSION. A Guide to the Reports on Collections of Manuscripts of Private Families, Corporations and Institutions in Great Britain and Ireland. 2 vols. in 3. London, 1914-38.

Not exhaustive. Indexes to individual reports must also be consulted.

855 CRICK, B. R., and MIRIAM ALMAN. A Guide to Manuscripts Relating to America in Great Britain and Ireland. London, 1961.

856 DE RICCI, SEYMOUR, and W. J. WILSON. Census of Medieval and Renaissance Manuscripts in the United States and Canada. 3 vols. New York, 1935-40.

857 American Literary Manuscripts: A Checklist of Holdings in Academic, Historical and Public Libraries in the United States. Austin, Texas, 1960.

858 HAMER, PHILIP M.   A Guide to Archives and Manuscripts in the United States. New Haven, 1961.

859 The National Union Catalog of Manuscript Collections 1959-1961. Ann Arbor, 1962.

For good lists of the catalogues of manuscripts at the English universities and other British libraries, see KENNEDY, Concise Bibliography (**15**), 4th ed., pp. 348-53. For printed guides to American collections, see DOWNS, American Library Resources (**287**).

Using and Editing Manuscripts; Textual Criticism

(The term "textual criticism" applies not only to manuscripts but to printed texts as well.)

863 BOWERS, FREDSON.   "Textual Criticism and the Literary Critic." Textual and Literary Criticism (Cambridge, 1959), pp. 1-34.

864 [POSTGATE, JOHN PERCIVAL.]   "Textual Criticism." Encyclopaedia Britannica, 11th ed., XXVI, 708-15.

865 [BOWERS, FREDSON T.]   "Textual Criticism." Encyclopaedia Britannica, 1960 ed., XXII, 13-18.

866 IVY, G. S.   "The Bibliography of the Manuscript-Book," in Francis Wormald and C. E. Wright, eds., The English Library before 1700 (London, 1958), pp. 32-65.

See also Harvard Guide to American History (**947**), pp. 88-104, for modern practices in the handling, editing, and printing of manuscripts.

PUBLIC RECORDS

871 GALBRAITH, V. H.   An Introduction to the Use of the [British] Public Records. Oxford, 1934.

> See also GALBRAITH'S Studies in the Public Records (London, 1948), Chapter 1.

872 GIUSEPPI, M. S.   A Guide to the Manuscripts Preserved in the Public Record Office. 2 vols. London, 1923-24.

873   See the article by Hilary Jenkinson in RAYMOND IRWIN, ed., The Libraries of London (London, 1949), pp. 55-91, for additional and more recent information on the Public Rec-

874   ord Office. This description may usefully be supplemented by The British Public Record Office (Richmond, Va., 1960) [Virginia Colonial Records Project, Special Reports 25, 26, 27].

For the Calendars of State Papers (Domestic and Foreign) and related calendars of English public records from the middle ages onwards—now totaling upwards of six hundred volumes—see the convenient list in MULLINS, Texts and Calendars (921), pp. 16-36.

---

875 Guide to the Records in the National Archives [of the United States]. Washington, 1948.

HISTORY: General

Handbooks and Encyclopedias

880 LANGER, WILLIAM L.   An Encyclopedia of World History. 3rd ed. Boston, 1952.

881 KELLER, HELEN REX.   The Dictionary of Dates. 2 vols. New York, 1934.

882 Haydn's Dictionary of Dates and Universal Information Relating to All Ages and Nations, ed. Benjamin Vincent. 25th ed. New York, 1911.

    First published 1841. Contents vary with each edition.

883 LITTLE, CHARLES E.   Cyclopedia of Classified Dates. New York, 1899.

884 MAYER, ALFRED.   Annals of European Civilization 1501-1900. London, 1949.

Histories

890 The Cambridge Medieval History, ed. H. M. Gwatkin et al. 8 vols. Cambridge, 1911-36.

891 The Cambridge Modern History, ed. A. W. Ward et al. 13 vols. Cambridge, 1902-11.

Now being supplanted in part by the following item.

892 The New Cambridge Modern History, ed. G. R. Potter et al. Cambridge, 1957- .

Fourteen volumes are projected.

Bibliographies

898 DUTCHER, GEORGE MATTHEW, et al. A Guide to Historical Literature. New York, 1931.

899 LANGLOIS, CHARLES-V. Manuel de bibliographie historique. 2nd ed. Paris, 1901-04.

900 International Bibliography of Historical Sciences [1926-]. Washington (later Paris, etc.), 1930- .

No volumes for 1940-46. The gap is partly filled by LOUIS B.
901 FREWER, Bibliography of Historical Writings Published in Great Britain and the Empire, 1940-45 (Oxford, 1947). See
902 also JOAN C. LANCASTER, Bibliography of Historical Works Issued in the United Kingdom, 1946-1956 (London, 1957),
903 and WILLIAM KELLAWAY, Bibliography of Historical Works Issued in the United Kingdom, 1957-1960 (London, 1962).

904 The American Historical Association's Guide to Historical Literature, ed. George Frederick Howe et al. New York, 1961.

HISTORY: English

Handbooks

908 POWICKE, SIR F. MAURICE, and E. B. FRYDE, eds. Handbook of British Chronology. 2nd ed. London, 1961.

909 HAYDN, JOSEPH, and HORACE OCKERBY. The Book of Dignities, Containing Lists of the Official Personages of the British Empire. 3rd ed. London, 1894.

Histories

915 The Oxford History of England. Oxford, 1934-62.

    I. R. G. COLLINGWOOD and J. N. L. MYRES. Roman Britain and the English Settlements. 2nd ed. 1937.

    II. F. M. STENTON. Anglo-Saxon England, c. 550-1087. 2nd ed. 1947.

    III. A. L. POOLE. From Domesday Book to Magna Carta, 1087-1216. 2nd ed. 1955.

    IV. SIR MAURICE POWICKE. The Thirteenth Century, 1216-1307. 2nd ed. 1962.

    V. MAY MCKISACK. The Fourteenth Century, 1307-99. 1959.

    VI. ERNEST F. JACOB. The Fifteenth Century, 1399-1485. 1961.

    VII. J. D. MACKIE. The Earlier Tudors, 1485-1558. 1952.

    VIII. J. B. BLACK. The Reign of Elizabeth, 1558-1603. 2nd ed. 1959.

    IX. GODFREY DAVIES. The Early Stuarts, 1603-60. 2nd ed. 1959.

    X. G. N. CLARK. The Later Stuarts, 1660-1714. 2nd ed. 1956.

    XI. BASIL WILLIAMS. The Whig Supremacy, 1714-60. 2nd ed. revised by C. H. Stuart. 1962.

    XII. J. STEVEN WATSON. The Reign of George III, 1760-1815. 1960.

    XIII. SIR LLEWELLYN WOODWARD. The Age of Reform, 1815-70. 2nd ed. 1962.

    XIV. R. C. K. ENSOR. England, 1870-1914. 1936.

Bibliographies

921 MULLINS, E. L. C. Texts and Calendars: An Analytical Guide to Serial Publications. London, 1958.

922 GROSS, CHARLES. The Sources and Literature of English History from the Earliest Times to about 1485. 2nd ed. London, 1915.

923 BONSER, WILFRID. An Anglo-Saxon and Celtic Bibliography (450-1087). 2 vols. Berkeley, 1957.

924 READ, CONYERS. Bibliography of British History: Tudor Period, 1485-1603. 2nd ed. Oxford, 1959.

925 DAVIES, GODFREY. Bibliography of British History: Stuart Period, 1603-1714. Oxford, 1928.

926 PARGELLIS, STANLEY, and D. J. MEDLEY. Bibliography of British History: The Eighteenth Century, 1714-1789. Oxford, 1951.

927 WILLIAMS, JUDITH BLOW. A Guide to the Printed Materials for English Social and Economic History 1750-1850. 2 vols. New York, 1926.

928 Writings on British History [1934-]. A Bibliography of Books and Articles on the History of Great Britain from about 450 to 1914, Published during the Year. London, 1937- .

As of 1962, coverage extended only through 1945. For material published in the United Kingdom since 1945, see **902**, **903**.

HISTORY: American

Handbooks

933 ADAMS, JAMES TRUSLOW, and R. V. COLEMAN. Dictionary of American History. 5 vols. and index. New York, 1942. Volume VI (Supplement One), ed. J. G. E. Hopkins and Wayne Andrews. New York, 1961.

934 Concise Dictionary of American History, ed. Wayne Andrews. New York, 1962.

935 MORRIS, RICHARD B. Encyclopedia of American History. Revised ed. New York, 1961.

Histories

940 MORISON, SAMUEL ELIOT, and HENRY STEELE COMMAGER. The Growth of the American Republic. 5th ed. 2 vols. New York, 1962.

Bibliographies

946 BEERS, HENRY PUTNEY. Bibliographies in American History. Revised ed. New York, 1942.

947 HANDLIN, OSCAR, et al. Harvard Guide to American History. Cambridge, Mass., 1954.

948 BASLER, ROY P., et al. A Guide to the Study of the United States of America. Washington, 1960.

949 Writings on American History [1902-]. Princeton, 1904; Washington, 1905- .

> Volumes for 1904-05 and 1941-47 were never published. Cumulative index, 1902-40.

Social History

England

955 TRAILL, H. D., ed.   Social England. 6 vols. London, 1893-97. Illustrated ed. 6 vols. London, 1901-04.

956 TREVELYAN, G. M.   English Social History. London, 1942.

> Also issued, with a wealth of illustrations, as Illustrated English Social History (4 vols., London, 1949-52, and 1 vol., London, 1956).

957 COULTON, G. G.   Medieval Panorama. Cambridge, 1938.

958 POOLE, AUSTIN LANE.   Medieval England. 2nd ed. 2 vols. Oxford, 1958.

959 [ONIONS, C. T., et al.]   Shakespeare's England. 2 vols. Oxford, 1916.

960 TURBERVILLE, A. S.   Johnson's England. 2 vols. Oxford, 1933.

961 [YOUNG, G. M.]   Early Victorian England, 1830-65. 2 vols. London, 1934.

America

967 SCHLESINGER, ARTHUR M., and DIXON R. FOX, eds.   A History of American Life. 13 vols. New York, 1927-48.

BIOGRAPHY

General

973 Biographie universelle ancienne et moderne. Nouvelle éd. 45 vols. Paris, 1843-65.

974 RICHES, PHYLLIS M.   An Analytical Bibliography of Universal Collected Biography. London, 1934.

975 Biography Index: A Cumulative Index to Biographical Material in Books and Magazines [1946-   ]. New York, 1947-   .

976 Chambers's Biographical Dictionary, ed. J. O. Thorne. Revised ed. New York, 1961.

For extensive lists of specialized biographical dictionaries and encyclopedias (artists, musicians, savants, etc.) and of such reference books for particular European countries, see MALCLÈS (494), I, 228-37.

English

978 Dictionary of National Biography, ed. Leslie Stephen and Sidney Lee. 63 vols. London, 1885-1900. (Later reprinted in 21 vols.)   (*"DNB"*)
   [First] Supplement. 3 vols. London, 1901.
   Errata. London, 1904. (For later corrections of *DNB* information, see cumulated index to Volumes I-XXV of the Bulletin of the [London University] Institute of Historical Research.)
   Second Supplement (3 vols., London, 1912) and succeeding decennial volumes (1927-59) contain articles on eminent persons who died 1900-50.

979 The Dictionary of National Biography: The Concise Dictionary.
   Part I . . . to 1900. Oxford, 1953.
   Part II: 1901-1950. Oxford, 1961.

980 BOASE, FREDERICK. Modern English Biography, Containing Many Thousand Concise Memoirs of Persons Who Have Died Since the Year 1850. 3 vols. Truro, etc., 1892-1901. Supplement, 3 vols. Truro, etc., 1908-21.

981 C[OKAYNE], G. E. The Complete Peerage of England, Scotland, Ireland, Great Britain and the United Kingdom, Extant, Extinct, or Dormant. New ed. 14 vols. London, 1910-59.

982 Burke's . . . Landed Gentry, ed. L. G. Pine. 17th ed. London, 1952.

983 Alumni Cantabrigienses: A Biographical List . . . from the Earliest Times to 1900, ed. John Venn and J. A. Venn. 10 vols. Cambridge, 1922-54.

984 Alumni Oxonienses: The Members of the University of Oxford [1500-1886], ed. Joseph Foster. 8 vols. London, 1887-92.

985 MATTHEWS, WILLIAM. British Diaries: An Annotated Bibliography of British Diaries Written between 1442 and 1942. Berkeley, 1950.

986 ————. British Autobiographies: An Annotated Bibliography of British Autobiographies Published or Written Before 1951. Berkeley, 1955.

ALLIBONE's Dictionary (39) contains biographical information on thousands of minor literary figures.

For valuable information on the genealogical aspects of biographical research relating to English figures, see ANTHONY
987 RICHARD WAGNER, English Genealogy (Oxford, 1960), Chapters VII-X.

American

991 Dictionary of American Biography, ed. Allen Johnson and Dumas Malone. 20 vols. and index. New York, 1928-37. Supplements One and Two. New York, 1944, 1958.   (*"DAB"*)
The supplements bring the record down to December 31, 1940.

992 KAPLAN, LOUIS. A Bibliography of American Autobiographies. Madison, Wis., 1961.

993 MATTHEWS, WILLIAM. American Diaries: An Annotated Bibliography of American Diaries Written Prior to the Year 1861. Berkeley, 1945.

994 DARGAN, MARION. Guide to American Biography. 2 vols. in 1. Albuquerque, 1949-52.

995 Appletons' Cyclopaedia of American Biography. 7 vols. New York, 1886-1900.

> Subsequently reprinted with excisions, 1915. Five supplementary volumes issued 1918-31.
>
> To be used with caution; contains an undetermined number of ghost biographies. See MARGARET C. SCHINDLER, "Fictitious Biography," American Historical Review, XLII (1937), 680-90.

996 The National Cyclopaedia of American Biography. New York, 1891- .

Some Books Every Student of Literature Should Read

In certain sections of this handbook, notably those on literary and cultural and intellectual history, are listed a number of works, like Matthiessen's *American Renaissance* and Lovejoy's *The Great Chain of Being*, which every student of literature should not merely refer to, but read. Here is a further selection of books, not so easily classifiable, the reading of which should be a part of one's education in modern tendencies in criticism, aesthetics, the history and theory of literature, and the history of ideas. Needless to say, the list is a sampling, and further titles will occur to every observer of contemporary literary thought.

AUERBACH, ERICH. Mimesis: The Representation of Reality in Western Literature. Princeton, 1953.

BARFIELD, OWEN. Poetic Diction: A Study in Meaning. 2nd ed. London, 1952.

BODKIN, MAUD. Archetypal Patterns in Poetry. London, 1934.

BOOTH, WAYNE C. The Rhetoric of Fiction. Chicago, 1961.

BURKE, KENNETH. The Philosophy of Literary Form. Baton Rouge, 1941.

ELIOT, T. S. Selected Essays. 3rd ed. London, 1951.

EMPSON, WILLIAM. Seven Types of Ambiguity. 3rd ed. London, 1953.

FEIDELSON, CHARLES, Jr. Symbolism and American Literature. Chicago, 1953.

FERGUSSON, FRANCIS. The Idea of a Theater. Princeton, 1949.

FORSTER, E. M. Aspects of the Novel. New York, 1927.

FRYE, NORTHROP. Anatomy of Criticism. Princeton, 1957.

GARDNER, HELEN. The Business of Criticism. London, 1959.

HOLLOWAY, JOHN. The Victorian Sage: Studies in Argument. London, 1953.

HYMAN, STANLEY EDGAR. The Armed Vision. New York, 1952.

LANGER, SUSANNE K. Philosophy in a New Key. Cambridge, Mass., 1942.

LEAVIS, F. R. The Common Pursuit. London, 1952.

LEVIN, HARRY. Contexts of Criticism. Cambridge, Mass., 1957.

LEWIS, R. W. B. The American Adam: Innocence, Tragedy, and Tradition in the Nineteenth Century. Chicago, 1955.

LOWES, JOHN LIVINGSTON. The Road to Xanadu: A Study in the Ways of the Imagination. Revised ed. Boston, 1930.

LUBBOCK, PERCY. The Craft of Fiction. London, 1921.

LUCAS, F. L. The Decline and Fall of the Romantic Ideal. New York, 1936.

MARTZ, LOUIS L. The Poetry of Meditation: A Study in English Religious Literature of the Seventeenth Century. (Yale Studies in English, CXXV.) New Haven, 1954.

ORWELL, GEORGE. Shooting an Elephant. London, 1950.

PRAZ, MARIO. The Romantic Agony. 2nd ed. London, 1951.

RANSOM, JOHN CROWE. The New Criticism. Norfolk, Conn., 1941.

RICHARDS, I. A. Principles of Literary Criticism. 5th ed. New York, 1934.

SMITH, HENRY NASH. Virgin Land: The American West as Symbol and Myth. Cambridge, Mass., 1950.

SPITZER, LEO. Linguistics and Literary History: Essays in Stylistics. Princeton, 1948.

TRILLING, LIONEL. The Liberal Imagination: Essays on Literature and Society. New York, 1950.

TUVE, ROSEMOND. Elizabethan and Metaphysical Imagery. Chicago, 1947.

VIVAS, ELISEO. Creation and Discovery: Essays in Criticism and Aesthetics. New York, 1955.

WILLIAMS, RAYMOND. Culture and Society 1780-1950. London, 1958.

WILLIAMSON, GEORGE. The Senecan Amble: A Study in Prose Form from Bacon to Collier. London, 1951.

WILSON, EDMUND. Axel's Castle: A Study in the Imaginative Literature of 1870-1930. New York, 1948.

A Glossary of Useful Terms

For further discussion of many of the terms found here, and of many more not included in this list, see Geoffrey Ashall Glaister, *Glossary of the Book* (London, 1960), John Carter, *ABC for Book Collectors* (3rd ed., London, 1961), and *The Bookman's Manual* (4th ed., New York, 1961), as well as books on analytical bibliography (752-755) and on historical method (22-23, 947).

A.L.S.   Autograph letter, signed; a letter wholly in the handwriting of its author. *L.S.* means a letter signed by its author but otherwise written by somebody else. *T.L.S.*—not to be confused with *TLS* (673)—means "typed letter, signed."

analytical bibliography   The branch of scholarship which, by examining such evidence as that provided by cancels, signatures, watermarks, and the like, attempts to establish the method by which a book has been manufactured. Cf. *descriptive bibliography*. See 750-755.

apocrypha   A work formerly—and doubtfully or mistakenly—attributed to an author is said to belong to his apocrypha. *The Testament of Love* is in the Chaucer apocrypha (it actually is by Thomas Usk), and *Arden of Feversham* is in the Shakespeare apocrypha. Cf. *canon, corpus*.

ascription   The conjecture, in the absence of definite proof, that a certain literary work was written by a given author. Thus *The Pricke of Conscience* once was, but no longer is, ascribed to Richard Rolle. Synonym: *attribution*.

association copy   A copy of a book once owned (or annotated) by the author himself, or by someone otherwise associated with the

119

book, such as the prototype of a character, or by some famous person. For example, the Folger Library has thousands of association copies of Shakespeare, once owned and in some cases annotated by people like Garrick, Johnson, Pope, Washington, Coleridge, Lamb, Emerson, Lincoln, Shaw, and General Tom Thumb. For an interesting demonstration of the importance of association copies in literary history and criticism, in this instance Browning's first copy of Shelley's poems, see Frederick A. Pottle, *Shelley and Browning: A Myth and Some Facts* (privately printed, Chicago, 1923).

attribution   See *ascription.*

author bibliography   A list of works by—often also works about— a certain author. These bibliographies vary enormously in authority, scope, and detail, from bare unannotated *check lists* (q.v.) to elaborate catalogues like Geoffrey Keynes's bibliography of John Donne (3rd ed., Cambridge, 1958) and Thomas J. Holmes's bibliography of Cotton Mather (3 vols., Cambridge, Mass., 1940).

bad quarto   A severely corrupted text of an Elizabethan play, usually transmitted by the memory of an actor or playgoer.

bibliographical ghost   A book that has never existed. Not to be confused with a book that actually was published, but all copies of which have disappeared. See George Watson Cole, "Bibliographical Ghosts," *PBSA*, XIII (1919), 87-112. There are also *biographical ghosts*, like those which haunt *Appletons' Cyclopaedia* (995). In modern reference works, ghosts are sometimes deliberately planted to forestall wholesale plagiarism; for example, in *Who's Who in America*, XXX (1958/9), the entry for "Hansell, Samuel G." is fictitious.

black letter   The heavy-faced type, often called "gothic," or, loosely, "Old English," in which many early books were printed. Beginning in England in the late sixteenth century, black letter was gradually replaced by roman (like this) and italic (*like this*).

calendar   A catalogue of manuscripts in a given collection, or by a particular author irrespective of location; lists date, place, addressee (if any), number of leaves and other physical details, and often gives a summary of contents. For examples, see the Reports of the Historical Manuscripts Commission or the Calendars of State Papers (above, pages 97 and 101). Also used as a verb: "to make a calendar."

call-number See *press-mark*.

cancel A substitute leaf or pasted-in slip, inserted in a book after it is printed (and in most instances bound), to eliminate a serious error of fact, or a blasphemy, a libel, a political heresy, or some other indiscretion. Also used as a verb: "to delete the offending matter and insert the replacement." The standard treatise on the subject, with numerous interesting examples, is R. W. Chapman, *Cancels* (London, 1930).

canon The total body of work accepted as by a certain author. Cf. *corpus*.

case See *font*.

catchword The first word on a new page as it is anticipatorily printed in the lower right hand corner of the preceding one. In old books, probably a device to help the printer arrange pages of type in the forme.

chain-lines In "laid" paper (which was used almost universally in books before the nineteenth century and is still found in some high-quality books), the widely spaced markings impressed into the paper by the wire mesh on which the pulp was dried. Chain-lines are spaced about three-quarters to one inch apart. (The closer-set lines which run crosswise are called *wire-lines*.) Because chain-lines always run parallel with the shorter dimension of the sheet to be folded, they are a valuable way of ascertaining the format of a book (running vertically in the leaf of a folio or an octavo, horizontally in a quarto). Not to be confused with *watermarks*.

check list A bibliography, generally somewhat tentative, whose entries are in simple form, without technical elaboration.

codex A manuscript volume; used especially of ancient and medieval texts. Plural: *codices*. Cf. *roll*.

collate (1) To compare two versions of a text, or two copies of a book, word by word or line by line. In its oldest form, simply a process of looking from one book to another and noting variations; in its most refined and complicated modern form, a highly mechanized process which has resulted in, among other things, the discovery of several hundred hitherto unnoticed variants in the text of Shakespeare. See Charlton Hinman, "Mechanized Collation at the Houghton Library," *Harvard Library Bulletin,* IX (1955), 132-34. (2) To analyze and describe the physical makeup of a book: format, number and designation of leaves, contents (dedication, preface, text, appendices, etc.), and presence of plates. For the best modern collation practices, see those followed in Greg's *English Printed Drama* (411).

colophon In older books, a note at the end giving such information as author, title, printer, and sometimes date of issue: "Thus endeth thys noble and Ioyous book entytled le morte Darthur . . . whiche book was reduced iu to englysshe by syr Thomas Malory knyght as afore is sayd and by me deuyded in to xxi bookes chapytred and enprynted and fynysshed in thabbey westmestre and the last day of Iuyl the yere of our lord MCCCCLXXXV Caxton me fieri fecit." In modern books, the term is sometimes used for the publisher's house-emblem or device: e.g., the Knopf borzoi, the Viking ship, the Holt owl, the Harper torch, the Macmillan monogram (opposite the title page in this book).

conflation A merging of variant texts into one. The editor assumes the responsibility of deciding which of the alternate readings are the closest to the author's intentions, and thus the readings to be adopted into what is, at best, an artificial reconstruction. A conflated text (sometimes called *eclectic*) has the same purpose as a *critical text.*

copy text The text of a work, in print or in manuscript, from which a new edition is set. More narrowly, the edition or manuscript which is closest to the author's intention and which is used as the basis for a critical edition. A classic discussion is W. W. Greg, "The Rationale of Copy Text," *Studies in Bibliography,* III (1950/51), 19-36. See *critical text.*

corpus The whole body of writings by a given author (in this sense the same as *canon*), or on a given subject.

corrupt Inaccurate, unfaithful to the original; used of any faulty literary text. See *bad quarto, critical text.*

critical bibliography A list of books with descriptive and evaluative annotations.

critical text (or **edition**) An authoritatively edited text of a work, usually based on the readings in the original manuscript, or the first edition, or the last edition corrected by the author. The critical text of a medieval work is based on a collation of manuscripts and the establishment of the best manuscript tradition, families of manuscripts, etc. In establishing a critical text—whether of a medieval or a modern work—the primary aim is to eliminate the corruptions (that is, the errors and gratuitous emendations) that have crept into the text since it left the hands of the author. The Manly and Rickert edition of *The Canterbury Tales* is critical in this sense; critical texts of Keats's poems have been made by Ernest de Selincourt and by H. W. Garrod. Cf. *conflation, recension, variorum edition.*

crux A word or passage in a text that is puzzling or does not seem to make sense; often blamed on careless typesetting or misreading of difficult handwriting. In many editions of Shakespeare, cruxes are marked by a cross-like dagger (†). Cf. *emendation.*

descriptive bibliography The branch of scholarship which, by analyzing and recording a book's title page, format, pagination, etc., can determine variant *editions, impressions,* and *issues* (qq.v.). Cf. *analytical bibliography.*

device A decoration, such as a shop-sign, crest, coat of arms, or emblem, which appears on the title page or final leaf of a book and identifies the book as the work of a certain printer or publisher. The precise state of a device in a given book—degree of wear, presence of small variations in the design, etc.—often affords a valuable clue to the date of printing. The standard guide is R. B. McKerrow, *Printers' and Publishers' Devices in England and Scotland, 1485-1640* (London, 1913). Cf. *colophon.*

document Any piece of manuscript (and, in the broadest usage, printed material as well) that contains information. Personal letters, diaries, legal papers, newspaper clippings, university records, laundry lists—all are documents. The collection of pamphlets and letters called "The Old Yellow Book" is the documentary source of Browning's *The Ring and the Book*.

duodecimo   A book made up of sheets folded into twelve leaves. This is more familiarly referred to as *twelvemo* and is abbreviated *12mo*.

eclectic text   See *conflation*.

edition   This is a term that has been, and is, very loosely used. In general, it designates all the copies of a book that are printed from one setting of type; the various printings may be spaced over months or years. A new edition is produced only when substantial changes have been made in the text (beyond a certain amount of minor revision), or when the type has been entirely reset. Cf. *impression, issue*.

emendation   An editor's correction of a reading in a text, to restore what he knows, or has reason to think, the author really meant to say. The most famous emendation in English literary history is the editor Theobald's alteration of Dame Quickly's description of the dying Falstaff in *Henry V* (II.iii.17)—"and a Table of greene fields"—to "and 'a babbled of green fields." Cf. *variant* (*reading*).

external evidence   Any evidence, apart from that found in the text itself, bearing upon authorship, date and circumstances of composition, sources, etc. of a literary work. Such evidence may consist of historical or biographical facts, or may be produced by physical analysis of manuscripts or printing practices, papers, inks, bindings, and the like. Cf. *internal evidence*. The most celebrated modern example of the use of both external and internal evidence, in this case to test the authenticity of literary documents suspected of being forgeries, is John Carter and Graham Pollard, *An Enquiry into the Nature of Certain Nineteenth Century Pamphlets* (New York, 1934).

extra-illustrated   See *grangerized*.

foliation   The numbering of a book's constituent parts by leaves rather than by pages: in printed books, a practice abandoned about 1600, but still retained in manuscript volumes.

folio (1) A large book made up of sheets folded only once. (2) The leaf of a manuscript or book (used chiefly of books lacking pagination). Abbreviated *f.* or *fol.* (plural: *ff.* or *fols.*).

font (British spelling: *fount*) In a printing house, a complete assortment of type of one style and size. For hand setting, each font is kept in a pair of shallow compartmented trays, called *cases*. The capital letters of type are kept in the upper tray and so are referred to as *upper case;* the small letters are kept in the lower tray and so are referred to as *lower case.* For specimens of various type faces see the University of Chicago *Manual of Style* (30).

format In bibliographical terminology, the physical makeup of a book as determined by the number of times each sheet has been folded (folio, quarto, octavo, etc.). In popular modern usage, all the physical features of a book, including the style of typography and binding. Note that in older library usage, and in current bookselling terminology, the terms *folio, quarto,* etc. designate the size of a book without relation to the number of times its sheets have been folded to make leaves. While it is true that a folio is the largest book, a quarto the next largest, and so on down to a virtually invisible 128°, these terms are only rough approximations, since there is wide variation in the size of the sheet. Hence the scientific bibliographer never uses them to refer to size except, perhaps, when talking with a bookseller.

forme A body of type laid out in a printer's *chase* or frame, comprising all the pages that will be printed on one side of a single sheet (two pages for a folio, four for a quarto, and so on). When the printed sheet is turned over and an equivalent number of pages printed on the blank side from another forme, it is said to be *perfected.* This book was printed 32 pages to a forme; a drugstore paperback is printed 64 pages to a forme.

front matter Everything preceding the main text of a book—title page, dedication, table of contents, foreword, preface, etc. Also called the *prelims.*

galley A long shallow tray in which composed type—about three pages' worth—is kept until it is divided into pages. From the standing type in this unpaged state *galley proofs* are "pulled."

gathering One section of a book, composed of the leaves into which a single sheet has been folded (or, in the case of a folio and occasionally of a quarto, more than one sheet—sometimes, also, half a sheet—is included). Approximate synonyms: *quire, signature* (sense 1).

ghost See *bibliographical ghost.*

grangerized Describes a copy of a book which has been "enriched" and often monstrously enlarged by the insertion of illustrations, autograph letters, and other material more or less related to the subject of the book. The term derives from James Granger, who published in 1769 a history of England, "with blank leaves for engraved portraits, etc." Boswell's *Life of Johnson* has often been thus treated; so also have histories of New England, topographical works, studies of Regency society, and other books of this sort. Synonym: *extra-illustrated.*

historical bibliography The historical study of papermaking, typefounding, illustration, printing, binding, publishing, bookselling, and allied arts and trades: the history of the book as a manufactured object and as an article of commerce. Cf. **750-778.**

holograph A manuscript wholly in the handwriting of its author. The word is also used as an adjective.

illumination The art, which reached its height in the middle ages, of decorating and illustrating manuscripts, particularly their initial letters and margins.

impression All copies of a book produced by a run of the sheets through the press at one time. Involves no fresh setting of type and therefore not to be called an *edition* (q.v.); an edition may consist of several impressions. Synonym: *printing.* Cf. *issue.*

imprint Publishing information (specifically, the name of the publisher or printer or both, accompanied by place of publication, and, usually, date) found at bottom of title page. Cf. *colophon.*

incipit The first line, especially of a medieval text; used to designate the text because there is no distinctive title. "Somer is comen wiþ loue to toune" is the first line, or incipit, of a poem in MS. Bodley

1687, f. 186ᵇ. "Indexes to first lines" in modern collections of poems are indexes to incipits.

incunabula (plural) Books printed before the year 1500. Singular forms: *incunabulum, incunable* (plural: *incunables*).

internal evidence The evidence produced by an analysis of a given text which throws light on its authorship, date, circumstances of composition, etc. Habits of literary style, imagery, and allusions to contemporary events are familiar kinds of internal evidence. Cf. *external evidence.* The validity of various kinds of internal evidence has been discussed in a lively symposium in the *Bulletin of the New York Public Library* (**655**), LXI-LXV (1957-61).

issue Those copies of an impression which differ from others of the same impression in that changes have been made after publication—chiefly those which alter some of the details of publication and sale, i.e., the title page and preliminaries. Cf. *cancel, edition, impression.*

leaf The smallest physical unit of a book, either side of which is a page. Thus the basic bibliographical equation: one leaf equals two pages.

lower case See *font.*

microtext An inclusive term for all processes by which books and manuscripts are reproduced in very small scale for reading through special machines. *Microfilm,* the oldest and most common process, involves the use of (generally) 35 mm. film, on each frame of which a single page or two-page opening is reproduced. A *microcard* (3 x 5 inches) contains a large number of pages of original text, photographically printed from microfilm. A *microprint* (6 x 9 inches) ordinarily contains about one hundred pages, printed (not photographically reproduced) from extremely tiny type. Immense quantities of research materials are now available in one or another of these forms; see for example entries for *STC* (**795**) and Evans (**822**), and the *Union List of Microfilms* (**322**) and *Newspapers on Microfilm* (**718**).

national bibliography A list of all books issued in a given country irrespective of author or subject.

octavo A book made up of sheets each of which has been folded three times to make eight leaves. Abbreviated *8vo* or *8°*.

offprint A copy of an article printed from the type used for its prior appearance in a journal or a book of multiple authorship. Distributing offprints or *separates* of one's published works to colleagues and fellow-specialists is a hallowed scholarly ritual.

O.P. "Out of print"; describes a book no longer available from the publisher. Differs from "out of stock," which implies that the shortage is temporary and that a new supply will be obtained from the printer.

page proof Proof pulled from standing type after it has been divided into pages. Cf. *galley*. Ordinarily the last chance the author has to make corrections before his work goes to press.

paleography The study of old handwriting, down to about the seventeenth century.

parchment The predecessor of paper, usually made from the skin of sheep or goats. Cf. *vellum*.

presentation copy A copy of a book that its author gave to someone else, as proved, usually, by an inscription in his own hand. An *inscribed copy*, on the contrary, bears no proof of being a gift; it may just as well have been purchased by the owner and signed by the author ("With best wishes, Benedetto Croce") at a department-store autographing party.

press-mark The letters and numbers that indicate a book's place on the library shelves. Synonym: *shelf-mark*. Both are British usage. American equivalent: *call-number*.

primary source Documentary testimony of the central figures, witnesses, or first recorders of an event; e.g., a contemporary chronicle, diary, or newspaper account. Cf. *secondary source*.

printing Synonymous with *impression*, q.v.

provenance The history of a particular volume or manuscript, especially the record of its successive owners. John Carter speaks of a fictitious volume known as "The Coningsby-Locksley Hall-Hent-zau-Casamassima-D'Urberville copy." For aids in tracing provenance, see **727-744.**

quarto A book made up of sheets each of which has been folded twice to make four leaves. Abbreviated *4to* or *4°* or *Q.*

quire See *gathering.*

recension This somewhat loosely used term, roughly equivalent to *version*, designates a re-working of a literary text by someone other than the author, with the implication of thorough revision rather than of incidental touching-up. Used especially, but not exclusively, in connection with Biblical and medieval texts.

recto The right-hand page of an open book. Hence "leaf A4^r" refers to the front of the fourth leaf in a gathering, or the seventh page. The page you are looking at is a recto. The back of a recto is a *verso.*

roll A document which, according to medieval English filing practice, was preserved by being rolled up rather than by being included in a volume (cf. *codex*). In the case of parchment membranes rolled up individually, *roll* is synonymous with *scroll;* more usually, however, particularly in government offices, membranes were sewn together end to end, forming rolls thirty or forty feet long.

rubric A note or heading in a manuscript, often in red (hence the name), giving information about the author, scribe, date or title, or any combination thereof. Medieval manuscripts did not have title pages; the rubric is the ancestor of the title page. The *colophon* (q.v.) was sometimes used as the concluding rubric.

running title The short title of a book or chapter which appears at the top of each normal page. By tracing the recurrence of each set of running titles, a bibliographer often learns how the book was printed, whether there were interruptions in the process, how many presses were used, and even the number of compositors.

scribal error A mistake in a manuscript attributed to the copyist, or *scribe.*

secondary source Documentary or other evidence which is not first-hand. Generally, a book, article, or other work which incorporates or purports to incorporate evidence found in *primary sources* (q.v.). John Stuart Mill's *Autobiography* (1874) is a primary source, Michael St. John Packe's *The Life of John Stuart Mill* (1954) is a secondary source.

serial In library usage, any work whose successive parts are issued at intervals, without any expectation of an end. The range is from weekly magazines to scholarly journals, reports of corporations, and the annals of learned societies. *The Year's Work in English Studies* (**454**), the *Bibliographic Index* (**504**), *PMLA* (**632**), and *Dissertation Abstracts* (**837**) are all serials. But the Yale edition of the letters of Horace Walpole, which will eventually be completed, is not.

sheet The large piece of paper that serves as a unit in book printing. Folded once, it provides two leaves or four pages (folio); folded twice, it provides four leaves or eight pages (quarto); folded three times, eight leaves or sixteen pages (octavo); and so on. The size was never standardized, but in Shakespeare's age, for instance, two very common sizes were 15 x 20 inches and 12 x 16 inches. This book was printed from sheets measuring 45 x 68 inches.

shelf-mark See *press-mark*.

signature (1) A printed sheet folded to constitute a unit of a book. Either alone or, in folios and some quartos, folded with one to three other sheets, equivalent to a *gathering* or *quire*. (2) The printer's mark, a letter, number, or symbol, which appears at the bottom of the recto of at least the first leaf of a sheet as folded. It guides the binder in assembling the folded gatherings in the right sequence (and the bibliographer in collating the book). Signatures in this latter sense are still regularly found in British books but seldom in modern books printed in the United States.

sixteenmo A book made up of sheets each of which has been folded into sixteen leaves. The common substitute for *sextodecimo;* abbreviated *16mo* or *16°*.

state A term used to differentiate variant copies of a book produced during a single press run and before the book has been offered for sale. Thus any textual changes during one pre-publication printing result in two or more states. To be differentiated from *issue,* q.v.

stationer The older term for a tradesman who published or sold books, or both (stationers also had many sidelines). A stationer might also be a printer, but often was not. Beginning in the sixteenth century the trade divided itself into printers, publishers, and retail booksellers; by the nineteenth century the word *stationer* came to refer almost exclusively to dealers in writing materials.

subject bibliography A list of books (and sometimes articles) about any subject. Relation to *author bibliography:* a list solely of books *about* a given author would be called a subject bibliography, but if it were added to one containing works *by* the author, the total product would be classified as an author bibliography.

textual criticism The branch of scholarship dedicated to examining critically the text(s) of a literary work, with the ultimate goal of determining as accurately as possible their origin, or their history, or what the author really wrote. Now closely connected with some phases of *analytical bibliography* (q.v.). See **863-865.** Cf. *critical text, recension.*

twelvemo See *duodecimo.*

uncut Describes a book the edges of whose leaves, though "opened," have not been trimmed down by the binder. Not to be confused with *unopened* (q.v.).

unique copy The only copy of a certain book that is known to exist.

universal bibliography A list of books with no limitations of subject, author, or time or place of origin.

unopened Describes a book whose leaves remain folded (closed) just as they were when the binder put together the component folded sheets. They have not been "opened" by the binder's shears or the reader's knife. A book that is *uncut* can be read; a book that is *unopened* cannot.

upper case See *font.*

variant (reading)   One of two or more different versions of a given word or passage in a work. Where one version is, for one reason or another, accepted as standard, the other version is often called the variant; but the term can be applied equally to either version. In *Hamlet*, I.ii.129, the Folio reads "O that this too too solid flesh would melt," while the First and Second Quartos read *sallied*. Or should it be emended to *sullied?* The controversy has raged ever since J. Dover Wilson argued for *sullied* (*What Happens in Hamlet*, Cambridge, 1935). An attractive variant reading in the General Prologue to *The Canterbury Tales* (line 386), adopted by two fifteenth-century scribes but not by fastidious modern editors, would place the Cook's running "mormal" where it belongs for maximum effect: not on his *shyne* but on his *chynne*.

variorum edition   An edition of a single literary work, or the collected works of an author, which contains a comprehensive collection of annotation and commentary by previous scholars. The term is also now used for an edition which attempts systematically to list all variant readings, both those found in contemporary manuscripts and editions and those proposed as emendations by later editors. Recent examples of variorums, in the latter sense, are editions of Yeats by Peter Allt and Russell K. Alspach (New York, 1957) and of Emily Dickinson by T. H. Johnson (Cambridge, Mass., 1955). The most famous example in English literature of a variorum which contains both textual variants and a copious selection of earlier commentary is the still unfinished *New Variorum Shakespeare*.

vellum   A fine grade of parchment made of calfskin.

verso   The left-hand page of an open book. This page is a verso. Opposite: *recto*.

watermark   The paper maker's trademark, sometimes a crude pictorial design, at other times one or more initials or words or a date, impressed into paper by twisted or soldered wires set into the screen on which the pulp is dried (cf. *chain-lines*). An important means by which scholars can approximately date, and sometimes establish the place of origin of, a book that is otherwise unidentified. See **756-758**. Also useful in helping to ascertain the format of a book. Until the end of the eighteenth century, the watermark was regularly placed in the center of one half of the sheet (as divided parallel with the shorter dimension). Thus the place where it appears in a gathering offers a clue as to how many times the sheet was folded.

wire-lines See *chain-lines*.

Xerox A new high-speed process by which any book (but, in practice, chiefly rare and out-of-print books) can be reproduced economically and conveniently. A microfilm is made of the text, and from the film is made an actual-sized reproduction of each page. These pages are then bound, to be handled and read like any other book.

Index

Authors, compilers, editors, titles, and subjects of all items in the numbered sequence are indexed. Unless otherwise indicated, references are to item numbers rather than to page numbers.

Yearbook of Comparative and General Literature, 65, 482
"Year's Contributions to Shakespeare Study, The," 462
Year's Work in English Studies, The, 454

Young, G. M., 961
Young, Karl, 169
YWES, 454

Zesmer, David M., 379